HBJ Reading Program

Margaret Early

Bernice E. Cullinan
Roger C. Farr
W. Dorsey Hammond
Nancy Santeusanio
Dorothy S. Strickland

LEVEL 7

Stairways

HBJ **HARCOURT BRACE JOVANOVICH, PUBLISHERS**
Orlando   San Diego   Chicago   Dallas

Acknowledgments

For permission to reprint copyrighted material, grateful acknowledgment is made to the following sources:

Curtis Brown, Ltd.: "Girls Can, Too" from *Girls Can, Too* by Lee Bennett Hopkins. Copyright © 1972 by Lee Bennett Hopkins. Published by Franklin Watts, Inc. Adapted from the second half of "The Galumpagalooses" by Eloise Jarvis McGraw. Copyright © 1983 by Eloise Jarvis McGraw. Originally published in *Cricket* Magazine.

Childrens Press: Adapted from *Sally Ride, Astronaut, An American First* by June Behrens. Copyright © 1984 by Regensteiner Publishing Enterprises, Inc.

John Ciardi: "How to Tell the Top of a Hill" from *The Reason for the Pelican* by John Ciardi. Copyright 1959 by John Ciardi.

Coward, McCann & Geoghegan: Adapted from *Nate the Great and the Missing Key* by Marjorie Weinman Sharmat. Text copyright © 1981 by Marjorie Weinman Sharmat.

Delacorte Press/Seymour Lawrence: "Dictionary" from *Laughing Time* by William Jay Smith. Copyright © 1953, 1955, 1956, 1957, 1959, 1968, 1974, 1977, 1980 by William Jay Smith.

E. P. Dutton, a division of New American Library: Adapted from *My Friend Jacob* by Lucille Clifton, illustrated by Thomas DiGrazia. Text copyright © 1980 by Lucille Clifton, illustrations copyright © 1980 by Thomas DiGrazia. Adapted from *The Balancing Girl* by Berniece Rabe, pictures by Lillian Hoban. Text copyright © 1981 by Berniece Rabe; illustrations copyright © 1981 by Lillian Hoban.

Greenwillow Books, a division of William Morrow & Company, Inc.: "The Cow" from *Zoo Doings* by Jack Prelutsky. Copyright © 1974, 1983 by Jack Prelutsky.

Harper & Row, Publishers, Inc.: "Rudolph is Tired of the City" from *Bronzeville Boys and Girls* by Gwendolyn Brooks. Copyright © 1956 by Gwendolyn Brooks. Complete text, abridged and adapted, and illustrations from *The Cloud*, written and illustrated by Deborah Kogan Ray. Copyright © 1984 by Deborah Kogan Ray.

Highlights for Children, Inc., Columbus, OH: From "City Grandfather, Country Grandfather" by Robert Hasselblad and adapted from "Thanks to Mary" by Ann Bixby Herold in *Highlights for Children*, February 1985. Copyright © 1985 by Highlights for Children, Inc.

Modern Curriculum Press, Inc.: Adapted from *The Mystery of Sara Beth* by Polly Putnam. Copyright © 1981 by Polly Putnam Mathews.

Pantheon Books, a division of Random House, Inc.: Adapted from *Big Boss! Little Boss!* (Titled: "Little Boss") by Barbara Bottner. Copyright © 1978 by Barbara Bottner. Adapted from *Backyard Basketball Superstar* by Monica Klein. Copyright © 1981 by Monica Klein.

Marian Reiner, on behalf of Kathleen Fraser: "Broom Balancing" from *Stilts, Summersaults and Headstands* by Kathleen Fraser. Copyright © 1968 by Kathleen Fraser. Published by Atheneum Publishers, Inc.

Russell & Volkening, Inc., as agents for Mary Ann Hoberman: "Brother" from *Hello and Good-by* by Mary Ann Hoberman. Copyright © 1959 by Mary Ann Hoberman. Published by Little, Brown and Company.

Scholastic Inc.: From *Akimba and the Magic Cow*, an African folktale retold by Anne Rose. Copyright © 1976 by Anne Rose.

Viking Penguin Inc.: Adapted from *Talking Without Words*, written and illustrated by Marie Hall Ets. Copyright © 1968 by Marie Hall Ets. From *Today Was a Terrible Day* by Patricia Reilly Giff. Copyright © 1980 by Patricia Reilly Giff.

Franklin Watts, Inc.: From *Jasper and the Hero Business* by Betty Horvath. Text copyright © 1977 by Franklin Watts, Inc. Published by Franklin Watts, Inc.

Albert Whitman & Company: From *Grandpa Retired Today* by Elaine Knox-Wagner. Text © 1982 by Elaine Knox-Wagner. Published by Albert Whitman & Company.

Key: (l)-Left; (r)-Right; (c)-Center; (t)-Top; (b)-Bottom

Photographs

Cover: Barry P. Fernald.
Page 2, Messerschmidt/Leo de Wys; 3, Shostal; 14, HBJ Photo; 15, HBJ Photo; 16 (all), HBJ Photo; 17 (all), HBJ Photo; 18, HBJ Photo; 44, HBJ Photo; 45 (all), HBJ Photo/Lloyd Hryciw; 46, HBJ Photo/Lloyd Hryciw; 47, HBJ Photo/Lloyd Hryciw; 48, Photri, Inc.; 59, Shostal; 62, Galen Rowell/FPG; 63, Wheeler Pictures; 86, NASA from Photri, Inc.; 87, NASA; 88, Wide World Photos; 89, NASA; 90, NASA from Photri, Inc.; 108, Index/Stone International, Inc.; 110, Jon Eastcott and Yva Momatiuk/The Image Works; 111, Robert H. Glaze/Artstreet; 125, Galen Rowell/FPG; 128, Ewing Galloway; 129 (l), Stan Ries/Leo de Wys; 129 (r), Richard Hutchings; 150, Camera Photo, Venice; 151, Musée National d'Art Moderne/Art Resource; 152, Musée National d'Art Moderne/Art Resource; 153, National Gallery of Art; 154, National Gallery of Art; 189, Stan Ries/Leo de Wys; 192–193, HBJ Photo/John Petrey.
Contents: Unit 1,2, Messerschmidt/Leo de Wys; Unit 2, 63, Wheeler Pictures; Unit 3, 129, Richard Hutchings; Unit 4, 192–193, HBJ Photo/John Petrey.

Printed in the United States of America

Continued on page 293

ISBN 0-15-330507-x

Contents

Unit 2 Mountaintops 62

Unit 3 # Bridges   **128**

Unit 4

Patterns

192

Stairways

Unit 1

Winding Roads

Have you ever walked down a winding road? If you have, you know that you can't see what is ahead. You aren't sure what will happen next. Maybe it will be funny. Maybe it will be exciting.

In each story in this unit, someone is doing something that is like going down a winding road. No one is sure what lies ahead.

As you read, think about the road each person takes. Think about how each person feels. Think about how you would feel if you were taking that same road.

Basketball season is about to start and Jeremy is faced with a problem. What is his problem and how does he solve it?

Backyard Basketball Superstar

by Monica Klein

All Jeremy could think about was basketball season. He thought about being captain of his team, the Flyers. Jeremy ran to read the big sign he had put in his front yard.

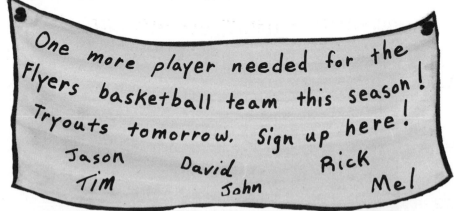

One more player needed for the Flyers basketball team this season! Tryouts tomorrow. Sign up here!

Jason   David   Rick
Tim   John   Mel

"Oh no!" he said. "It can't be! I don't believe it!"

Just then Micky and Adam rode by. "Hi, Jeremy!" said Micky. "How many names are on the list?"

"One too many," said Jeremy. "The last one on this list is *my little sister*!"

"But she can't play basketball," said Adam.

"Just take a look in my backyard," said Jeremy. They all ran to the backyard. They watched Melanie make basket after basket.

"She can play!" said Micky.

"Not on *my* team!" said Jeremy.

"She's taller than anyone on the team," said Adam.

"She's not just tall," said Micky. "She jumps high and runs fast, too."

"She sure can throw a basketball," said Adam, "even if she is a girl."

"She's not just a girl," said Jeremy. "She's my little sister, and she can't play on my team!"

"We'll see you tomorrow," said Adam as he and Micky left.

"Melanie!" Jeremy called. "I bet you're tired, aren't you?"

"Boy, am I ever!" said Melanie.

"Well, since you're so tired, I'll clean your room," said Jeremy.

"You will?" said Melanie.

"Sure," said Jeremy, "and since you're so tired, you won't want to try out for the Flyers tomorrow."

"What?" said Melanie. "I'll be in great shape by tomorrow. I wouldn't miss the tryouts for anything!"

"Not even for my giant ant farm?" asked Jeremy.

"Jeremy, I'm getting the idea that you don't want me to try out for the Flyers," said Melanie.

"I never said that," said Jeremy.

"Don't worry, Jeremy," said Melanie. "You'll be proud of me. I'll play my best at the tryouts."

"I know you will," said Jeremy.

"That's what I'm worried about," Jeremy thought to himself.

7

Jeremy went inside. He heard Melanie in the yard. *Swish thump! Swish thump!*

"Why does *my* little sister have to be a backyard basketball superstar?" he said to himself. "When Melanie tries out for the team, all the Flyers will laugh at me."

Jeremy sighed and said to himself, "A backyard basketball superstar in my own family, and it's not me."

The next morning everyone met in Jeremy's yard. "Jeremy!" said one of the Flyers. "Your sister wants to try out. You're our captain. Can a girl try out?" Everyone waited for Jeremy's answer.

Jeremy did not say a thing. He thought about being captain and being the best team on the block. He knew what he had to do. He took the ball and threw it into Melanie's hands. "Shoot, Mel," he said. *Swish thump! Swish thump!*

"She sure is good," said Micky.

"Even if she is a girl," said Adam.

"She's not just a girl," Jeremy thought to himself. "She's my little sister! But—she is just the player the Flyers need to be the best team on the block."

After everyone had a chance to try out, Jeremy said, "Let's vote!"

Each of the Flyers wrote a name on
a slip of paper and put it in a box.
Then Jeremy opened the box and read
the names.

"We all voted for the same person,"
Jeremy said.

"We did?" said Micky.

"Even you?" asked Adam.

"Yes," said Jeremy. "We all voted
for the one person who can run fast,
jump high, and really throw a
basketball. Welcome to the Flyers, Mel!"

Melanie smiled. She threw the ball
into the basket. *Swish thump!* The
players all knew it would be a very
good basketball season.

1. What was Jeremy's problem, and how did he solve it?

2. Why didn't Jeremy want Melanie to try out to play for the Flyers?

3. What makes you think that Jeremy was really proud of his sister?

4. How did Jeremy help his team become the best team on the block?

5. What words are used to show that Melanie shoots baskets well?

Pretend you are Melanie. Write three sentences telling Jeremy why you should try out for the team. Or pretend you are Jeremy. Tell why you think Melanie should not try out.

Girls Can, Too!

by *Lee Bennett Hopkins*

Tony said: "Boys are better!
  They can . . .

    whack a ball,
    ride a bike with one hand,
    leap off a wall."

I just listened
  and when he was through,
I laughed and said:

"Oh, yeah! Well, girls can, too!"

Then I leaped off the wall,
  and rode away
With *his* 200 baseball cards
  I won that day.

Exercising can be fun. What are some exercises you can do? Why are these exercises good for you?

"E" Is for Exercise

by Nanette Mason

What exercises do you do? Do you know that when you walk fast, run, swim, or ride your bike, you are really exercising? Do you know that when you jump rope or play tag, you are also exercising?

Do you want to run faster? Would you like to jump higher or throw a ball better? Here are some more exercises that are fun to do and good for you, too.

These exercises will help you move better and help make your body strong. Always begin with stretching exercises to help you warm up. Numbers 1–4 are stretching exercises. Numbers 5–7 will help make your body strong.

1. Stand up. Bend down to touch your toes.

2. Sit with your legs out. Reach past your toes.

3. Sit with one leg out. Bend the other leg back. Reach out and try to touch your toes.

4. Stand with your feet flat on the floor. Lock your hands behind your neck. Turn slowly left, then right.

5. Stand with your feet flat on the floor. Then raise and lower your heels.

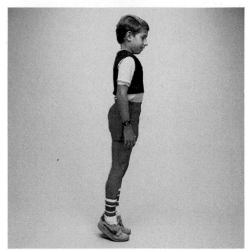

6. Lie on your back. Bend your knees. Keep your feet flat on the floor. Lock your hands behind your head. Sit up and touch your elbows to your knees.

7. Pull yourself up on
an exercise bar, or
hang from it.

When you exercise, the last thing you should do is cool down. Give your body a chance to cool down slowly by doing some more stretching exercises.

If you exercise every day, you will feel good, look good, and be stronger.

1. What are three exercises that you read about?

2. Why are exercises good for you?

3. What is the last thing you should do after exercising?

4. Which exercise could be called "sit-ups"? Find that part of the selection.

Exercise will help you feel good, look good, and be strong. Write a paragraph that tells about something else you can do that will help keep your body strong.

Contents Page

Suppose you want to learn more about exercising. You find two books that you could read. The title of one book is *Exercising for a Stronger You*. The other title is *Why Should You Exercise?* You can decide which book to read by looking at the Contents page of each one.

Look at the Contents pages below. Read the chapter titles. These titles tell what each chapter is about.

<table>
<tr><td colspan="2">Exercising for a Stronger You</td><td colspan="2">Why Should You Exercise?</td></tr>
<tr><td colspan="2" align="center">━━ CONTENTS ━━</td><td colspan="2" align="center">━━ CONTENTS ━━</td></tr>
<tr><td>Chapter</td><td>Page</td><td>Chapter</td><td>Page</td></tr>
<tr><td>1. Exercising the Parts</td><td>3</td><td>1. Who Needs Exercise?</td><td>3</td></tr>
<tr><td>Legs</td><td>4</td><td>Babies and Children</td><td>7</td></tr>
<tr><td>Arms</td><td>5</td><td>Grown-ups</td><td>12</td></tr>
<tr><td>Upper body</td><td>7</td><td>Older People</td><td>15</td></tr>
<tr><td>2. Getting Stronger</td><td>10</td><td>2. What Parts are Helped?</td><td>20</td></tr>
<tr><td>How Soon Does It Work?</td><td>13</td><td>Help for Bones</td><td>23</td></tr>
<tr><td>How Often to Do It?</td><td>16</td><td>Help for Lungs</td><td>25</td></tr>
<tr><td>How Long Each Time?</td><td>19</td><td>Help for Skin</td><td>26</td></tr>
</table>

Notice that under each chapter title are **subtitles.** The subtitles tell more about what is in each chapter.

Suppose you want to find out if your grandmother should exercise. Which book would you read? Why? Did you say *Why Should You Exercise?* Chapter 1 of this book is called "Who Needs Exercise." One subtitle under this chapter title is "Older People." So, this book would be the one you should read.

Suppose you decided to find out if exercising every day is good for you. Which book would you use? Why? Did you say *Exercising for a Stronger You*? Chapter 2 of this book is called "Getting Stronger." One subtitle is "How Often to Do It." So, this book is the one you should read.

When you want to learn what is in a book, you should read more than the book title. You should also read the chapter titles and the subtitles on the Contents page.

Ronald can't seem to do anything right today. What surprise does Ronald get at the end of this day?

Today Was a Terrible Day

by Patricia Reilly Giff

Today was a terrible day. It started when I dropped my pencil. Miss Tyler asked, "Ronald Morgan, why are you crawling under your desk like a snake?" So all the children started to call me Snakey.

When Miss Tyler told us to take out last night's homework, I noticed that my mother had forgotten to sign mine. I quickly signed it for her. Miss Tyler said, "Ronald Morgan. It is wrong to sign other people's names. Besides, you spelled your mother's name wrong." All the children laughed.

Later, when Billy was reading—he's in the Satellite group—I got hungry. I was so hungry that I tiptoed to the coatroom and ate a sandwich. I had the wrong bag, however, so I ate Jimmy's sandwich.

"Ronald Morgan, what are you eating?"
Miss Tyler asked.

"A sandwich," I said. "I ate Jimmy's
sandwich by mistake."

All the children looked at me. Jimmy
cried because he didn't want my sandwich.

Then, when Alice was reading—she's in
the Mariners—my group had to do a
workbook page. I didn't remember how to
do it so I asked Rosemary.

"Don't you even know how to do that?"
Rosemary asked. She's in the Rockets
group, just like me.

Later, we went outside to play ball. I
played left field because I don't catch very
well. Only one ball came near me. I ran
for it. I almost had it.

I missed, and my milk money fell out of my pocket. "You just lost the game, Snakey," Billy yelled.

When lunchtime finally came, I had no money for milk. I watched Jimmy eat my sandwich. I was still hungry. All I had was part of Rosemary's carrot and one of Billy's grapes.

After lunch, Miss Tyler called the Rockets to the reading circle. I'm a Rocket. Rosemary read the first sentence. Tom read the next one. They didn't make any mistakes today.

When it was my turn, I said, "Sally was a horse." I was almost sure I hadn't made a mistake.

Miss Tyler said, "Ronald Morgan, you made a mistake."

Rosemary said, "Sally saw a house."

Tom said, "Some Rocket you are."

It was almost time to go home. Miss Tyler said, "I think the plant person has forgotten to water the plants again." Guess who the plant person is?

I got up and watered all the plants. While I was doing the last one, the best one, I looked out the window. Somehow I knocked the pot off the windowsill.

When it was finally time to go home, Miss Tyler gave me a note. "Ronald Morgan," she said. "Take this note home. Try to read it by yourself. If you can't, I'm sure your mother will help you."

On the way home, I read the note.

Guess what? I read that whole note by myself without making any mistakes. I can read. Wait till I tell Michael. He's my best friend.

"Hello, Michael? This is Snakey. Guess what? I just found out I can read. Guess what else? It's Miss Tyler's birthday tomorrow. I think I'll take her a plant. I know she needs one."

1. What surprise did Ronald get at the end of the day?

2. Tell three things that made Ronald's day a terrible one.

3. What did Miss Tyler do to make Ronald feel better?

4. How did you feel when you read Miss Tyler's note to Ronald? Why?

5. When did you begin to think that Ronald's next day might be better?

Think about Ronald's terrible day. What might make a school day terrible for you or a friend? Write a paragraph telling what could happen and when, where, and why it could happen.

Sequence

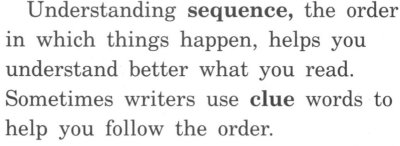

Understanding **sequence,** the order in which things happen, helps you understand better what you read. Sometimes writers use **clue** words to help you follow the order.

Read the paragraph below. Use the underlined clue words to help you understand the sequence.

Tim thinks he is ready to go to school. <u>Before</u> he leaves, his mother wants him <u>first</u> to eat his cereal and <u>then</u> to walk the dog. <u>After that</u>, Tim can go to school.

Did you notice the clue words *before, first, then,* and *after that*? These clue words should help you answer some questions about the sequence, or the order in which Tim is to do things.

What is Tim to do first? He is to eat his cereal. How do you know? The clue words are *before* and *first*. What is Tim to do next? He is to walk the dog. How do you know? The clue word is *then*. What is Tim to do last? He is to go to school. How do you know? The clue words are *after that*.

Now look for clue words as you read the following paragraph.

Bill's mother left a note for him. The note said, "First, clean your room. Then I want you to go to the store. Please cut the grass after that. You can go swimming later."

Did you find the clue words *first, then, after that,* and *later?* Now answer the following questions and tell how you know. What is Bill to do last? What is Bill to do second? What is the third thing Bill is to do?

Remember, clue words will help you understand better the sequence, or the order in which things happen.

Margaret has a good idea for the school carnival. What is her idea? How does her idea help the school?

The Balancing Girl

by Berniece Rabe

Margaret was very good at balancing. She could balance a book on her head. She could wheel along in her wheelchair as nice as you please. The book would not fall off.

One day Margaret balanced thirty blocks on the floor. "That's simple," Tommy said.

"Then you do it," said Margaret.

Tommy wouldn't try. He just said, "I still say it's simple."

Margaret planned and planned. She wanted to do something very special that Tommy could not call simple. She got out of her wheelchair. She pushed some other chairs together. She made a private corner for her work. It took a long time and great care, but at last she was finished. She had finished a fine castle of blocks.

Tommy said, "That's simple. I build castles like that all the time."

Margaret would have shouted at him, but Ms. Joliet said, "Time for recess."

When they came back into the room after recess, Margaret's castle was knocked down flat!

Tommy was the first person to shout, "I don't know who did it!"

Ms. Joliet had to leave the room just then. It gave Margaret a chance to say, "Tommy, you had better never knock down anything I balance again, or *you'll be sorry*!"

When Ms. Joliet came back, she said, "We are going to hold a school carnival to raise money. We need ideas."

Quickly Tommy raised his hand. "My dad and I could run a fishpond booth. People would pay to fish for prizes." Everyone clapped for Tommy's idea.

"Good," said Ms. Joliet. "Are there any other ideas?"

At the end of the day, Ms. Joliet said, "Each of you put on your thinking cap. See if you can come up with a good idea for the carnival by tomorrow."

Well, it was no trouble at all for Margaret to balance a thinking cap on her head. She thought and thought. The next morning, she said something quietly into Ms. Joliet's ear.

Again Margaret made a private corner. Deep in the corner, she started setting dominoes on end. She placed each domino just a small space away from the last one. She had to be so very, very careful. If anything touched a domino and made it fall, then one by one they would all come falling down.

She soon used all the dominoes, so the next day Ms. Joliet got some more for her. Everybody watched while Margaret made a whole city.

Margaret never saw who dropped a pencil right in the middle of her city. She moaned. "I can't reach into the middle to get it out. One slip and my whole city is gone!"

"I'll get it," said Tommy.

Ms. Joliet stopped him just in time. "I will do it, Tommy." The whole class held their breath. Even Ms. Joliet held her breath as she reached into the middle and got the pencil.

The next day, Margaret finished placing the last domino. Everyone wanted to be the one to push down the first domino. Margaret said, "The name of the person to do that will be pulled out of a hat on the last night of the carnival, *and* you will have to pay to get your name in that hat."

The school carnival was really great. Margaret went to every booth. Then it was time to go to Margaret's corner. A voice said, "Let's move along to the second grade room and see who gets to push down that first domino."

Ms. Joliet waited until everyone was close to Margaret's corner. Then she let the oldest child in the room draw the name from the hat. There wasn't a noise in the room.

Ms. Joliet read,

Tommy pushed to the front. He stepped inside the domino corner. He stood there just looking at Margaret. "Well, push," said Margaret.

Tommy pushed much harder than was needed, but still it went beautifully. Click, click, click. The dominoes took their turns falling. It seemed to take forever for them all to fall. Then a big cheer went up!

Tommy looked right at Margaret and yelled, "There! I knocked down something that you balanced, and I'm not sorry."

"I know you're not," Margaret called back. "Guess what? I made the most money in this whole carnival."

"Hooray! Hooray for the Balancing Girl!" someone shouted. Margaret was sure she heard Tommy join in the big cheer.

1. What was Margaret's idea for the school carnival?

2. How do you know that her idea was a good one?

3. How did Tommy upset Margaret?

4. How did you feel when the pencil was dropped in the domino city? Why?

5. What words on page 38 made you think that people wanted to find out who got to push down the first domino?

Put on your "thinking cap." Think about something you can do well. Write a paragraph that tells what you can do and how you learned to do it.

42

Broom Balancing

by Kathleen Fraser

Millicent can play the flute
and Francine can dance a jig,
but I can balance a broom.

Susanna knows how to bake cookies
and Harold can stand on one foot,
but I can balance a broom.

Jeffry can climb a ladder backwards
and Andrew can count
   to five thousand and two,
but I can balance a broom.

Do you think a circus might discover me?

43

Margaret used dominoes to build a city. Read to find out other ways dominoes can be used.

What Can You Do with Dominoes?

by Linda Beech

People have been playing with dominoes for a very long time. No one knows just how old dominoes are, but they were used long, long ago in China.

Most domino sets have 28 pieces. The pieces are small and flat. They are almost always black and white. The pieces can stand on edge.

One side of each domino has nothing on it. The other side has two parts. The parts may have small white dots on them, or they may be blank. The dots are called *pips*. This side is used for playing games.

4 pips  **2 pips**

6 pips

The highest number of pips on one piece is 12. That piece has six pips on each part. A piece that has the same number of pips on each part is called a *double domino*. This piece is the double six.

6 pips

double six

The lowest number of pips on a domino is one. This piece has one pip on one part, and the other part is blank.

blank  **1 pip**

One domino in each set has no pips. This is the double blank.

double blank

45

Many different games can be played with a set of dominoes. Most people play the block game. In this game, the dominoes are placed on a table with the pip side down. Each player takes five pieces. The rest of the dominoes are left in the pile on the table. The players do not show their pieces to the other players.

The player with the highest double domino goes first. That domino is put on the table pip side up. Suppose the first domino is the double three. The next player must play a domino that has three pips on one part. If the player does not have such a piece, then that player must pick from the pile of dominoes until a matching piece is found.

Suppose the second player plays the three-five piece. The third player must use a piece with three or five pips.

2nd player   **1st player**

Look at the picture. What piece did the third player use?

3rd player   **2nd player**   **1st player**

Now look at the next picture. It shows how the third player would have played using a piece with three pips on one part.

1st player

2nd player   **3rd player**

Notice that double dominoes are always placed in a different way from the other pieces.

As the game goes on, each player tries to match one part of a domino to another. All the players try to be the first to use their pieces.

Some people like to build things with dominoes. Then they like to watch them fall down. If dominoes are set up in rows, they fall down in rows, too,—one by one, faster and faster.

The men in the picture used dominoes to make big words and pictures. It took them many weeks to set up the dominoes. Then, with just a small tap, they pushed the first domino. Down went the dominoes, row by row by row!

1. Tell three ways in which dominoes can be used.

2. Tell how the game of dominoes is played.

3. Do you think that this game would be fun to play? Why?

4. What did you read that told you that dominoes is an old game? Find that part of the selection.

Think about your favorite game. Write a paragraph that tells about that game. You may also tell how to play the game or why you like that game.

49

Today is a very special day for Grandpa. What makes this day so special? How does Grandpa feel about this special day?

My Grandpa Retired Today

by Elaine Knox-Wagner

My Grandpa retired today. I was the only kid at the party. "Come have some juice, Margey," Grandpa said. So I did. We never have juice at the barbershop. It was very good.

Then I oiled the barber chairs and moved them up and down. I swept up black hair and brown hair and a little red hair.

Grandpa was talking and laughing with all the men. I pulled on his arm. "Should I wash the combs?" I asked.

"Not yet. Why don't you throw out all the old newspapers," he said. I saluted. He saluted. It's an old game we play.

I threw the old newspapers into the trash can. I wiped off all the cans and bottles and lined them up.

Grandpa stood in a circle of tall
men. Some I didn't even know. I stood
on a chair and waved at him over
their heads. He waved back. I slipped
through the circle and took Grandpa's
hand. He smiled at me. His friends
smiled at me.

Grandpa's friend, Joe, slapped him on
the back. "Well, Al," he said, "time
for the big surprise."

"Tata-ta-ta!" someone yelled. We all
turned to look.

Someone had tied a giant red bow around the barber chair with Grandpa's name on the back. "Because no one can take your place, Al, we want you to take this chair with you," said Joe. Everyone clapped. Grandpa just stared.

Soon the men were gone, the "Closed" sign was in the window, and Grandpa's barber chair was driving away in the back of a truck.

"Well, let's give the place a last clean-up, then," he said. We filled some of the bottles. We put the combs in to be washed. We did everything we could think to do. At last, it was time to leave.

"Do you want to lock up?" Grandpa asked.

"You do it today," I said.

We walked home slowly. I kicked a
stone and sighed. Grandpa kicked a
stone and sighed. We waited for a
green light.

"This might be fine weather for the
beach," Grandpa said.

"I like barbershops," I said. The light
changed.

"Then again, we always did mean to
get downtown to see those dinosaur
bones," he said.

"You can see them in books," I said.

Grandpa took my hand. "I sure will
miss the shop," he said.

"Me, too," I said.

When I went to say good night, Grandpa was in his room, sitting in the barber chair that said "Al" on the back. His eyes were closed, and he looked lonesome. I climbed onto his lap. "There is more to life than working in a barbershop," I said.

Grandpa laughed and laughed and laughed. So I laughed and laughed and laughed. "I don't know where you pick up some of the things you say," he told me.

"From you, mostly," I said.

"Off to bed with you now," he said. "We've got things to do tomorrow."

1. What made the day special for Margey's grandpa?

2. What special thing did Grandpa's friends do with his barber chair?

3. Will Margey and Grandpa miss the barbershop? How do you know?

4. How did Margey help Grandpa feel better? What else could she have done to help?

5. When did you learn why the chair was given to Grandpa?

Think about what Margey and Grandpa can do now that he is retired. Pretend you are Margey. Write a paragraph telling some things you and he can do.

Thinking About "Winding Roads"

In the stories you have just read, you met people on many different roads. These people did not know what they would find as they started, but they went ahead anyway.

Mel and Jeremy each tried something new, and it turned out just fine. Ronald was having a terrible day, but on his way home from school he discovered that he could read. Margaret would not let anything stop her from trying a new road. At first, Grandpa and Margey weren't sure that they would like their lives after Grandpa retired.

As you read other stories, think about how people sometimes find themselves on a winding road. Think about how the people in the stories face new things in their lives.

1. How are Melanie and Margaret the same? How are they different?

2. Was Ronald's day like Margey's day? Why?

3. Do you think Tommy from "The Balancing Girl" would be good friends with Jeremy from "Backyard Basketball Superstar"? Why?

4. Which person in this unit followed the most interesting winding road? Why do you think so?

Read on Your Own

Running with Rachel by Frank and Jan Asch.
Dial. A girl talks about why she started
to run, how to pick out the right shoes,
what exercises to do, and much more.

Timothy and Gramps by Ron Brooks.
Bradbury. A young boy doesn't like
school because he is lonely. After his
grandfather visits school, he begins to
enjoy it more.

Big Shoe, Little Shoe by Denys Cazet.
Bradbury. A young rabbit wants to help
his grandfather do his job. His helping
doesn't work until they change places.

Next Year I'll Be Special by Patricia Reilly Giff.
Dutton. Marilyn dreams about how
things will be better when she's in
second grade. She thinks everything
will be perfect.

The Crack-of-Dawn Walkers by Amy Hest. Macmillan. Every other Sunday, Sadie and Grandfather take a special walk.

The Adventures of Albert, the Running Bear by Barbara Isenberg and Susan Wolf. Clarion. Albert escapes from the zoo and finds himself running in a marathon.

How to Make Snop Snappers and Other Fine Things by Robert Lopshire. Greenwillow. Learn how to make games, toys, and crafts.

Games (and How to Play Them) by Anne Rockwell. Harper. This book tells how to play forty-three games.

Alexander and the Terrible, Horrible, No Good, Very Bad Day by Judith Viorst. Atheneum. Nothing goes right and everything goes wrong for a young boy.

Unit 2

Mountaintops

Do mountains have a special meaning for you? Do you think you would like to climb a mountain? Why?

Some people say they have reached a mountaintop when they feel very good about something they have done. In each story in this unit, someone has reached a goal or solved a problem. Each person feels good about something.

As you read, think about the goals the characters reach or the problems they solve. Think about how they feel when they reach their mountaintops.

Jasper wants something very much.
Does Jasper get what he wants?
If so, how does he do it?

Jasper and the Hero Business

by Betty Horvath

Jasper lived in the house on the corner. It was a busy corner. All day long people passed by, hurrying to work and then hurrying home again.

Jasper didn't hurry. He didn't have any place to go. Sometimes he didn't have anything to do. He just sat and watched the people pass by. Sometimes people stopped and talked to Jasper. They asked him questions.

There was one question that everybody asked him. "Jasper, what are you going to be when you grow up?"

"I'm going to be a hero," Jasper said. Then the people laughed. "Wait and see," thought Jasper. "Someday I am going to be a big hero. I will have my picture in the paper."

One day Jasper's brother Paul said, "All right, Jasper the Hero, I have a job for you."

"This is no job for a hero," said Jasper. He carried out the trash anyway. Then he went back inside the house to wait for something brave to do.

A fire truck went clanging by. "There goes a hero," said Jasper. "That fire fighter is off to do brave deeds and help people in trouble."

That night the newspaper had a picture of a fire fighter. He was carrying a baby he had saved. Jasper cut the picture out of the paper. That's the way his hero board began. Every time Jasper read about someone being brave, he pinned the story to the board on his bedroom wall.

"Someday," said Jasper, "my picture will be up there, too." He was saving a place for it.

"There is never anything dangerous going on around here," said Jasper.

"That's good," said his mother. "Let's keep it that way."

Jasper took Rover for a walk. He saw somebody running down the street. "Maybe there has been a robbery," Jasper thought. "Maybe this is a robber coming! When he gets closer, Rover and I can catch him. Maybe Rover will even bite him!"

As the runner got closer, Jasper saw that it was Mr. Brown out doing his jogging. Mr. Brown patted Rover's head. Rover wagged his tail. "Nothing dangerous here," thought Jasper.

Jasper turned the corner. Right there on the ground was a piece of paper. It was money! "If I can't be brave," said Jasper, "it's good to be rich."

As Jasper got to the next corner, he heard somebody crying. It sounded as if someone were in trouble or even in danger! "Here's my chance to be a hero," said Jasper.

He saw a little boy who was crying. "Are you lost?" Jasper asked. "Can I take you home?" Jasper could see the headlines in the newspaper. "Hero Finds Lost Child."

"No," sobbed the little boy, "*I'm* not lost. My money's lost."

Jasper sighed. "I found some money," he said. "I guess it's yours."

The little boy took the money. He didn't say anything. He just watched Jasper and Rover go into the house.

"Maybe I'm going about this hero business all wrong," thought Jasper.

"Do you know any heroes?" he asked his mother.

"Look out the window," said his mother. "There is a hero coming up the walk this very minute."

Jasper ran to the window. "That's just Father," he said. "I never knew he was a hero."

"There are all kinds of heroes," said his mother. "Your father worked hard today to earn money to pay the rent and the food bill. Maybe he would have liked to do something else."

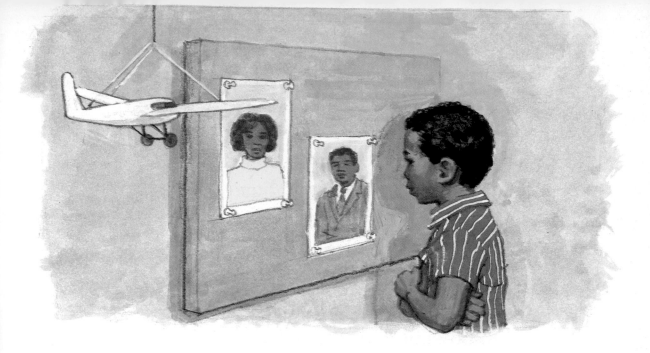

"Then I will put his picture on my
hero board," said Jasper. Jasper put a
picture of his father on his hero board.
Then he pinned his mother's picture next
to it. There was still the place where
Jasper's picture belonged. He was getting
older every minute. Another day was
almost gone. Jasper wasn't a hero yet.

While they were eating supper, the
doorbell rang. Jasper's father answered
the door and came back carrying a bunch
of flowers. "These are for you," he said.

"Jasper has a girlfriend!" said Paul.

"No," said his father, "it was a little
boy. He said Jasper gave him money."

"Oh, *him*!" said Jasper. "I *found* some money, but it was his. So I just gave it to him."

Nobody said anything for a minute. Then Paul said, "I bet that little boy thinks Jasper is a hero."

"Who, me? A hero?"

"Sure," said Paul. "If somebody thinks you're a hero, you are one. It is time to pin your picture on the hero board."

Paul helped him pin the picture on the board. Under it they wrote "Jasper the Hero." The board was finished now. There was no more space. "Now that you are a hero," said Paul, "what are you going to be next?"

"You don't ever stop being a hero," said Jasper, "but maybe I'll be something else, too. I think I'll be a hero and work on being a doctor. What are you going to be?"

"Me?" asked Paul. "I'm going to be busy trying not to get sick!"

1. What did Jasper want to be?

2. How did Jasper become a hero to the little boy?

3. Name three people who were heroes in the story.

4. How do you feel about Jasper's brother? Why?

5. When in the story did Jasper learn that there are different kinds of heroes?

Think

and

Write

Pretend you are Jasper. Write a paragraph that tells about some other good deeds that you could have done to become a hero.

Newspapers

People read newspapers to find out what is happening in other countries or at home. They may want to know about last night's ball game, tomorrow's weather, or tonight's television shows. You can read about many different things in a newspaper.

The Hometown News

Hometown, Any State   *May 20, 1999*

INDEX

NEW STAR FOUND IN SPACE

The first page of the newspaper has the name of the paper and the date. It also has the name of the city and state where the newspaper is printed. On the first page are the stories that most people want to read.

A newspaper is divided into parts. Each part has special kinds of stories. On the first page of the newspaper is an **index.** The index tells you the name of each special part and the page where you will find that part. Look at the newspaper index on page 74.

Suppose you want to read about the baseball game you saw on television. What part would you read? Did you say "Sports," on page 8?

Suppose your mother asks you to find the part that tells what time a special show will be on television. What page will you find for her?

Newspapers are filled with interesting stories. The index on the first page helps you find the stories you want to read.

Nate is a detective who has a case to solve. What clues does Nate use as he tries to solve this case?

Nate the Great and the Missing Key

by Marjorie Weinman Sharmat

I, Nate the Great, am a detective. I am not afraid of anything, except for one thing. Today I am going to a birthday party for the one thing I am afraid of—Annie's dog, Fang.

This morning my dog Sludge and I were getting ready for the party. The doorbell rang. I opened the door. Annie and Fang were there. "I need help," Annie said. "I can't find the key to my house. I can't get in to have the birthday party for Fang."

76

I, Nate the Great, was sorry about the key and glad about the party. I said, "Tell me about your key."

"Well," Annie said, "the last time I saw it was when I went out to get Fang a birthday surprise to eat."

"To eat?" I said.

"Yes," Annie said. "That's the one present I had forgotten to buy. I got Fang lots of presents. I got him a new collar with a license number, a silver name tag, and a little silver bone to hang from the collar. See how pretty Fang looks."

I, Nate the Great, did not want to look at Fang. "Tell me more," I said.

"Well, Rosamond and her four cats were at my house," Annie said. "When I went to the store, I left Rosamond and the cats in my house. I left Fang in the yard. I left the key to my house on a table. That is the last time I saw the key. When I got back, Fang was still in the yard, but the house was locked. Rosamond and her cats were gone. Rosamond left this note."

Your key can be found
At a place that is round
A place that is safe
And where things are shiny.
A place that is big
Because it's not tiny.
And this is a poem.
And I went home.

"That is a strange poem," I said.

"Sometimes Rosamond is strange," Annie said.

I, Nate the Great, knew that. "You must ask Rosamond where she put your key."

"I went to her house," Annie said. "No one was home."

I, Nate the Great, said, "I will take your case."

I wrote a note to my mother.

Dear Mother,

I am on a case.
I am looking for a
round, safe, shiny, big
place. When I find it,
I will be back.

Love,
Nate the Great

Annie, Fang, Sludge, and I went to Annie's house. "What does your key look like?" I asked.

"It is silver and shiny," Annie said. Sludge and I looked around. There were many places to leave a key. They were not round, safe, shiny, and big.

"I will have to look in other places," I said.

"Fang and I will wait for you here," Annie said. I, Nate the Great, was glad to hear that.

Sludge and I started walking. All at once I saw a big, safe place. It was a bank. I knew there were many round, shiny things in a bank. Sludge and I walked inside.

BANK

"Do you want to put some money in the bank?" the guard asked.

I said, "Did anyone strange with four cats leave a key here?" The guard pointed to the door. Sludge and I left.

Now I, Nate the Great, knew where I should not look for the key. A bank was not a strange enough place for a strange person like Rosamond to leave a key.

I sat down to rest beside a trash can. I had an idea. A trash can would be a strange enough place for Rosamond to hide a key! Now I, Nate the Great, knew that I had to look in Annie's trash can.

Sludge and I walked to the trash can behind Annie's house. I tried to pull up the cover. Sludge tried to push up the cover with his nose. I pulled harder. Sludge pushed harder. We looked inside the can. There was nothing there.

I, Nate the Great, had not solved the
case. Sludge and I went home.

I was very hungry. I made pancakes.
I sat down to eat them, but I did not
have a fork. I opened a drawer. It was
full of spoons and knives and forks all
together in a shiny silver pile. I had to
look in the drawer a long time before I
found a fork. It is hard to find something
silver and shiny when it is mixed in with
other things that are silver and shiny.

I, Nate the Great, thought about that.
Maybe Annie's key was someplace where
nobody would see it because it was
with other shiny silver things. Now I,
Nate the Great, knew the place!

Sludge and I went back to Annie's house. "I know where your key is," I said.

"Where?" Annie asked.

"Look at Fang's collar," I said.

Annie looked. "I see Fang's license hanging on his collar," she said. "I see his silver name tag. I see his silver bone and—my key!"

"Yes. I, Nate the Great, say that Rosamond hung your key on Fang's collar. We did not notice it because there were other silver things there."

"But why did Rosamond hang it there?" Annie asked.

I said, "That's easy. Remember
Rosamond's poem? Well, Fang's collar is
round. The things hanging on it are shiny.
Fang is big. There is no place more safe
to leave a key than a few inches from
Fang's teeth. No one would try to take off
that key, not even me." I started to leave.

"Wait!" Annie said. She took the key
from Fang's collar. "Now I can have my
party, and you can come!"

I, Nate the Great, was glad for Annie
and sorry for me. We all went inside.
Annie gave me the best seat because I
had solved the case. It was next to Fang.
I, Nate the Great, hoped it would be a
very short party.

1. What are some clues that Nate used to find the missing key?

2. How did Nate feel about Fang? How do you know this?

3. Why did Rosamond write a poem?

4. How did you feel about where Nate sat at Fang's party?

5. What did you read on page 80 that made Nate think that the bank was a good place to look for the key?

Rosamond hid the key in a good hiding place. Think about another good hiding place. Write a paragraph that tells where it is and why it is a good hiding place.

Sally Ride wanted to circle the earth, and she did. Read to find out what she has to say about that trip.

Sally Ride, Astronaut — An American First

from a book by June Behrens

5 . . . 4 . . . 3 . . . 2 . . . 1 . . . 0 . . . Lift-off! Spacecraft *Challenger* lifted off from Cape Canaveral, Florida. Up into the air it climbed. In a few minutes, it was out of sight.

This was *Challenger*'s second trip into space. One of the five astronauts on this flight was Sally Ride. Sally was the first American woman to go into space. She was also the youngest American astronaut to circle the earth.

While in space, each astronaut had important work to do. Sally Ride's job was to test a robot arm. She was to find out how well the arm worked. This was the first time the robot arm was to be used in space. On later trips, the arm would be used to pick up satellites in trouble.

Challenger's second flight lasted six days. Then the spacecraft returned to Earth. It landed in California.

Sally Ride had grown up in California
not far from where *Challenger* landed.
While Sally was growing up, she worked
hard to be good at whatever she did.
Sally had always been interested in
the stars and planets. She studied
about them in school.

One day Sally read in the newspaper that men and women were wanted for the space program. They would learn to be astronauts. Many, many people wanted to be part of the space program. However, only thirty-five were picked for the 1978 astronaut class. Sally Ride was one of the six women picked.

Sally moved to Texas to begin her training as an astronaut. She learned to fly airplanes. She learned about flying a spacecraft. She learned to work the robot arm. Sally learned all the things an astronaut needs to know.

U.S. AIR FORCE T-38A NO-80
A.F. SERIAL NO. 69-7084
SERVICE THIS AIRCRAFT WITH GRADE
JP-4 FUEL IF NOT AVAILABLE T.O. NO
42B1-1-14 WILL BE CONSULTED FOR

1. PUSH
2. PULL

The very best astronauts were needed for the second *Challenger* flight. These people would have to work as a team. Sally Ride was picked as part of the second *Challenger* team. This team worked very hard to get ready for the flight.

On June 18, 1983, the whole world watched as *Challenger* lifted off. Sally Ride made news.

"The thing that I'll remember most about the flight is that it was fun. In fact, I'm sure it was the most fun that I'll ever have in my life," said Sally Ride.

1. How did Sally Ride feel about her trip into space?

2. Why was Sally picked as part of the *Challenger* team?

3. Why is Sally Ride an American "first"?

4. How did you feel when Sally was picked to go into the astronaut class? Why?

5. What did you read on page 89 that made you think that other people wanted the same job as Sally?

Think about what job you would like when you grow up. Write a paragraph telling what the job is and why it would be a good job for you.

Each time Akimba thinks he has solved his problem, Bumba, his neighbor, tricks him. How does Akimba trick Bumba?

Akimba and the Magic Cow

An African folktale, retold by Anne Rose

Akimba was the poorest man in his village. One morning he had nothing left to eat—not even a crumb. "I have no food and I have no money. I must leave the village," Akimba thought, "and see what I can do."

Akimba set out. Soon he came to a deep forest. He saw an old man chopping firewood. Akimba helped him stack the logs. "Where are you going?" the old man asked.

"I have no food and I have no money. I must see what I can do," Akimba said.

"Maybe I can help you," said the old man. "Behind this bush you'll find a cow. Take her home with you and say 'kukuku.' Say 'kukuku' to her and see what happens."

Akimba took the cow and went back to his hut. "Kukuku," he said to the cow. The cow opened her mouth and a gold coin fell out. "Wah!" cried Akimba. "Kukuku! Kukuku!" In no time at all, Akimba was rich.

One day Akimba had to go on a long trip. He could not take his cow with him. He went to see his good neighbor Bumba. "Bumba," he said, "will you keep my cow for me? She's no trouble as long as you don't say 'kukuku' to her. 'Kukuku' is the one thing you must never say."

"Very well," Bumba said. "I will do as you wish."

Akimba gave Bumba the cow and went down the road. The very moment Akimba was gone, Bumba ran up to the cow. "Kukuku," he said. To his surprise the cow opened her mouth and a gold coin fell out. "Kukuku," Bumba said again. Another coin fell to the ground. "Wah!" cried Bumba. "This cow is good to have and better yet to keep."

A few days later, Akimba came back. "Where is my cow?" he asked.

"Here she is," Bumba said, but he gave Akimba another cow instead.

Akimba took the cow home and said, "Kukuku."

"Moo-oo," mooed the cow. Nothing happened.

"Have you forgotten your owner's voice?" Akimba shouted. "Kuku, kukuku!"

"Moo-oo, mooo-ooo," mooed the cow.

Akimba went to find the old man in the woods. "My cow stopped giving gold," Akimba said. "Soon I will be hungry again."

"Behind this bush, you'll find a sheep. Take her home with you and say 'bururu.' Say 'bururu' to her and see what happens."

Akimba took the sheep and went back to his hut. "Bururu," he said to the sheep.

The sheep opened her mouth and a silver coin fell out. "Wah!" Akimba shouted. "Bururu, bururu!" In no time at all, Akimba was rich.

The day came when Akimba had to leave on another trip. He brought his sheep to his good neighbor Bumba. "Bumba," he asked, "will you keep my sheep for me? She's no trouble as long as you don't say 'bururu' to her. 'Bururu' is the one thing you must never say."

"Very well," Bumba said. "I will do as you wish." The moment Akimba was gone, Bumba ran over to the sheep. "Bururu!" he said. The sheep opened her mouth. A silver coin fell out.

"Wah!" Bumba shouted. "This sheep is good to have and better yet to keep."

A few weeks later, Akimba came back. "Where is my sheep?" he asked.

"Here she is," said Bumba, but he gave Akimba another sheep instead.

Akimba hurried home. "Bururu," he said to the sheep.

"Baa, baa," said the sheep. Nothing happened!

"Bururu! Bururu!" Akimba shouted.

"Baa, baa, baa," said the sheep.

"This sheep has turned deaf while I was away," said Akimba.

Again Akimba went to find the old man in the woods. "My sheep stopped giving silver," he said. "Soon I'll be hungry again."

"There is a chicken behind this bush. Take her with you," said the old man. "When you get home, say 'klaklakla' to the chicken. Say 'klaklakla' and see what happens."

Akimba got the chicken and took her home. "Klaklakla," he said to her. The chicken laid an egg. "What?" yelled Akimba. "No silver? No gold?"

"Klaklakla," Akimba shouted again. The chicken laid more eggs. "Well," said Akimba, "eggs are eggs." Then he ate them.

The next time Akimba was called away, he asked Bumba to keep his chicken. "She's no trouble as long as you don't say 'klaklakla' to her. 'Klaklakla' is the one thing you must never say."

"Do not worry," Bumba said. "I will be more than glad to keep your chicken." As soon as Akimba was out of sight, Bumba ran to the chicken.

"Klaklakla!" he shouted. The chicken laid an egg. "Fooh!" cried Bumba. "No gold? No silver? Only eggs? Oh well, eggs are eggs." Then he ate them.

When Akimba came back and asked for his chicken, Bumba gave him another chicken instead. Akimba hurried home. "Klaklakla," Akimba said to the chicken, but nothing happened.

Akimba went to find the old man in the woods again. "My cow stopped giving gold," he cried. "My sheep stopped giving silver. Even my chicken stopped laying eggs. Soon I will be as hungry as before."

"There's a stick behind this bush," the old man said. "Go home and tell it to dance for you. Shout 'mulu' when you want it to stop."

"Thank you," said Akimba, and he took the stick.

As soon as he was home, Akimba told the stick to dance, but the stick did not dance. It jumped up and beat him instead. Akimba was so surprised he almost forgot the magic word. "Mulu!" he yelled at last, and the stick fell to the floor.

Akimba looked at the stick for a long time. "Humm," he thought. "I must pay another visit to Bumba."

Then Akimba took the stick to Bumba's house. "Bumba," he said, "I have to leave again. Will you keep my stick for me?"

"Well, well," Bumba thought. "The cow brought me gold. The sheep brought me silver. The chicken brought me eggs. Who knows what the stick will bring?" He grabbed the stick and pushed Akimba out the door.

Akimba turned around. "I almost forgot," he said. "Do not say 'Stick, dance for me.' Remember, whatever you do, do not ask the stick to dance."

The moment Akimba was out of sight, Bumba yelled, "Stick, dance for me!" The stick jumped up, but it did not dance. It beat Bumba and beat him and would not stop. The stick was still hitting him when Akimba came back.

"Now will you give me my true cow and my true sheep and my true chicken?" Akimba asked.

"Anything!" cried Bumba. "Just stop this stick from beating me!"

"Mulu," Akimba said. The stick fell to the floor. Akimba picked up the stick. He took his true cow and his true sheep. He took his true chicken. Then he went back to his hut.

"Klaklakla," Akimba said to the chicken. His plate was filled with eggs. "Bururu," Akimba said to the sheep. Silver coins clanked to the floor. "Kukuku," Akimba said to his cow. Gold coins piled up to the roof. Akimba never had to go hungry again.

1. How did Akimba trick Bumba into giving back his true things?
2. In what way was Akimba not wise?
3. Why didn't Akimba give Bumba the magic word to stop the stick?
4. How did you feel when the stick was beating Bumba? Why?
5. When in the story did you first think that Akimba had a plan for getting his true animals back?

Think and Write

Think about being a good friend. Write a paragraph that tells what you think a good friend should do and how you think a good friend should act.

The Cow

by Jack Prelutsky

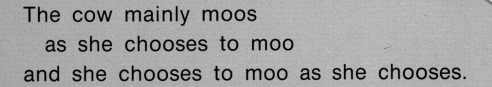

The cow mainly moos
   as she chooses to moo
and she chooses to moo as she chooses.

She furthermore chews
   as she chooses to chew
and she chooses to chew as she muses.

If she chooses to moo
   she may moo to amuse
or may moo just to moo as she chooses.

If she chooses to chew
   she may moo as she chews
or may chew just to chew as she muses.

Main Idea and Details

The sentence in a paragraph that tells what all the other sentences are about is called the **main idea.** The other sentences in a paragraph give **details** about the main idea.

Read the following paragraph. Find the main idea and three details that tell about the main idea.

There are many kinds of parades. Some parades are held to celebrate New Year's Day. Some parades tell you that the circus is in town. Some parades welcome heroes home.

The main idea is that there are many kinds of parades. The other sentences give details about three kinds of parades.

The main idea of a paragraph is not always in the first sentence. Find the main idea and two details in the paragraph below.

Sally Ride learned to fly a spacecraft. She learned to work the robot arm. She learned everything an astronaut needs for a space flight.

The first two sentences in this paragraph give details. The last sentence tells the main idea.

Now read this paragraph to find the main idea and the details.

The parade was called off because of the rain. Children could not go out to play. The wet grass couldn't be cut. The rain kept people inside.

What is the main idea? What are the details? How do you know?

Remember, looking for the main idea and details will help you understand better what you read.

Each day you see clouds in the sky. Read to find out what clouds are and how they are formed.

Cloudy Weather

by Anne Maley

If you were up in space, you could see Earth floating like a big ball. If you came closer, you could see the clouds that cover Earth. If you came closer still, you could see that Earth is made of land and water.

Have you ever wondered what makes the clouds above Earth? The answer is in the air around you.

Water in the Air

The air is a wonderful collector. It collects bits of dust and smoke. Most of all, it collects water. As it moves over Earth, the air takes water from oceans and lakes. It also takes water from plants and soil. Did you know that the air even collects water from *you*? Here is one way it happens.

Suppose you are wet from swimming. You sit down to dry. As the sun dries you, it turns the water on your body into a gas called water vapor. The water vapor floats into the air, like tiny bubbles you can't see. As the bubbles float higher and higher, they grow colder and colder. When they become cold enough, the bits of vapor turn back into drops of water. Each drop forms around a tiny bit of dust. Many drops of water cling together to form a cloud.

Clouds in the Sky

Clouds are everywhere in the sky. Some are very high in the sky. Some float in the middle of the sky. Others are closer to the ground. The highest clouds are the coldest ones. These clouds are made of little bits of ice.

One good place to look for a cloud is on top of a mountain. Can you guess why you might find a cloud there? The answer is that air always grows colder as it moves up the side of a mountain. When the air reaches the top of the mountain, the water vapor has become little drops of water that form a cloud.

As the sun shines on this cloud, the cloud looks warm and bright. If you were to climb through a cloud, though, it would feel cold, dark, and very wet.

Clouds on the Ground

Did you know that you could walk through a cloud without climbing a mountain? When you walk in fog, you are in a cloud that is on the ground.

When air is filled with water, it is called heavy air. Fog may form when heavy air near the ground cools. The water vapor in the air turns into big drops of water or ice. When the sun warms the air, the fog goes away.

Clouds and the Weather

Each kind of weather has its own kind of clouds. Some people read the clouds to guess what kind of weather is coming. How good are you at reading clouds? Do you know that white, puffy clouds high in the sky often mean good weather? Dark, puffy, flat-bottomed clouds low in the sky often mean rain.

When it rains, the clouds give back much of the water the air has collected. The water soaks into the ground. It fills oceans and lakes. It makes puddles. Soon the puddles go away again. Where do they go?

You know the answer to that question!

1. What are clouds, and how are they made?

2. Water is in the air. Name three things that can make this happen.

3. What are two places where clouds can be found?

4. What did you learn about heavy air?

5. How many parts does this selection have? What tells you this?

Think and Write

Pretend you are a cloud looking down on Earth. Write a paragraph that tells how things look on Earth when you are floating in the sky. One thing might be that cars look like ants crawling on the ground.

How to Tell the Top of a Hill

by John Ciardi

The top of a hill
Is not until
The bottom is below.
And you have to stop
When you reach the top
For there's no more UP to go.

To make it plain
Let me explain:
The one *most* reason why
You have to stop
When you reach the top—is:
The next step up is sky.

In "Cloudy Weather", you read about how clouds are formed. As Nina and her mother climb a mountain, they walk through a cloud. What does Nina discover about the cloud?

The Cloud

Story and pictures by Deborah Kogan Ray

The sky was orange behind the mountain when Nina woke up. She listened to the forest sounds around her. "What will we see on our walk, Mama?" asked Nina.

Her mother answered, "I can't really say, Nina. Every walk is different. We're going to walk all the way up this mountain. We're going to walk so high into the sky that we might even walk right into a cloud."

Nina thought about what it would be like to walk in a cloud. Maybe the cloud would be as soft as a pillow.

Nina looked at the steep hill. It seemed so high. She wondered how they would ever be able to climb such a steep hill.

They crossed a stream and started to climb up the path. They climbed higher and higher. The path went around and around and up. Nina's legs hurt. She felt hot and sticky. She thought she might cry.

Mama stopped. She wiped Nina's face. "You're a real climber, Nina. We just went all around the mountain. It's just a little farther to the top."

They climbed higher and higher still. They climbed past the tall trees. Finally, they reached the top of the mountain.

"Wow, did we ever walk far up," Nina said. "There must be a lot of clouds to walk in, way up here." She looked up at the sky, but she didn't see any clouds. There was no wind. Nothing moved.

Nina looked way down. A valley stretched far below. When she looked toward one end of the valley, she saw trees that looked as small as baby plants. Past the trees she saw a lake that looked like a tiny puddle of water.

When Nina looked toward the other end of the valley, she saw something strange. It looked like a giant white pillow. "Look, Mama. What's that?"

"That's a cloud," Mama answered.

Nina wondered about the way it looked. She had seen lots of clouds before. "It doesn't look like a cloud. It's not in the right place. It should be up in the sky. It shouldn't be under us," she said.

"It is in the sky, Nina. We've just climbed so high we're over the clouds."

"Is that cloud coming our way? Will I be able to walk in it?" Nina asked.

"I think so," Mama said. "That cloud is blowing this way pretty fast. We are going to walk down the path into the valley to get to that lake."

Nina looked. The cloud was almost right under them. "I can't wait," she said. The cloud looked cottony soft.

Mama led her back to the path. They started to walk down the mountain. The path was very rocky. Nina shivered. "When will we be in the cloud, Mama?"

"We are in the cloud now," Mama said. "It's blowing a lot of cold air on us."

"We can't be in that cottony white cloud," Nina said. "This is cold and ugly." Nina looked back. All she could see was gray mist. She shivered again and put her hands into her pockets.

"I don't like this. I'm cold, Mama." Nina shook her head. "This isn't pretty. This isn't what I see when I look at the sky. Inside the cloud should look nice. It shouldn't feel this way."

Nina wished the walk would end.

Mama said softly, "Come on, Nina. Let's stay warm together." Mama put her arm around Nina.

They walked down the path on the side of the mountain. Down and down they went, into the valley. "Now the trees are keeping the cloud from blowing the cold air on us," said Mama. The air felt warmer. The sky grew lighter.

"I didn't think the cloud would be like it was when we were walking down the mountain," Nina said. "I was scared, Mama."

Mama kissed Nina. "I know you were, Nina."

"Now the cloud is so pretty," Nina said. She held out her hands in the floating mist. She walked away from Mama. "Look, Mama," she laughed. "I'm walking in a cloud."

1. What did Nina think the cloud would be like? Why?

2. What did Nina discover about the cloud?

3. What two things made Nina unhappy?

4. How did you feel about Nina when she was afraid?

5. When in the story did you first begin to think that Nina would not like the cloud?

Think about a special place to which you would like to go. Write a paragraph that tells where you would like to go and what you would like to do or see while you are there.

Thinking About "Mountaintops"

You have just read about people who reached a goal or solved a problem. Each person felt very good about something he or she had done. Remember that we sometimes say that a person who feels this way has reached a mountaintop.

Jasper found that he could be a hero right at home. Nate used clues to solve the problem of the missing key. Akimba had help, but he finally solved his problem and had enough money for the rest of his life. Sally Ride became a hero in space. Nina climbed a real mountain.

As you read other stories, think about how the people in the stories are trying to reach a goal or solve a problem. Think about how you would feel if you were in their place.

1. What might Jasper think of Sally Ride? Why?

2. How might the story "Akimba and the Magic Cow" have been different if Nate the Great had been in Akimba's place?

3. How are Sally Ride and Nina the same? How are they different?

4. Which person in this unit had the hardest mountaintop to reach? Why do you think so?

Read on Your Own

Bringing the Rain to Kapiti Plain by Verna Aardema. Dial. This is an African folktale about a cowherd who brought rain to the very dry plain where he lived.

Fast and Slow: Poems for Advanced Children of Beginning Parents by John Ciardi. Houghton. This book includes thirty-four funny poems such as "I Should Never Have Trusted That Bird."

The Cloud Book by Tomie dePaola. Holiday. This book tells about the ten most common clouds and what they can tell us about the weather that's coming.

Girls Can Be Anything by Norma Klein. Dutton. A girl and a boy are pretending that they're different people. The boy discovers that a girl can be a doctor, a pilot, or even President.

Weather by David Lambert. Watts. This book tells all about weather. Find out about rain, snow, clouds, and storms.

The New Kid on the Block by Jack Prelutsky. Greenwillow. This book has funny poems about such strange creatures and people as Baloney Belly Billy.

Fog Drift Morning by Deborah Kogan Ray. Harper. In this book a mother and daughter gather blueberries at the seashore on a misty morning.

Nate the Great and the Snowy Trails by Marjorie Weinman Sharmat. Coward. Rosamond's birthday gift for Nate disappears. Nate solves the mystery.

Weather Experiments by Vera Webster. Childrens Press. This book tells how to do ten weather experiments.

Unit 3

Bridges

You know that bridges help us get from one place to another. Did you know that bridges are also ways for us to reach out to other people?

When we meet someone who is different from us, we say that we need a bridge of understanding. By this we mean that we need a way to help us get to know others.

As you read the stories in this unit, think about the bridges people have built to other people. Think about why these people needed to build a bridge of understanding.

Do you think it is better to be a big sister or a little sister? What do Penny and Lizzie decide?

Little Boss

by Barbara Bottner

"I can't wait until next week," yelled Lizzie.

"I can," said Penny. "Everyone is making such a big fuss over you. Mother is making a big fuss. Father is making a big fuss. You are making the biggest fuss of all, just because next week is your birthday."

"Being six is important," said Lizzie.

"Well," Penny said. "Someone else is having a birthday next week, too. Me! Penny! I'll be eight!"

"Eight is too old to make a fuss over," Lizzie said.

"That's the trouble," said Penny. "Nobody is even making a little fuss, just because I'm the big sister."

"Okay, I'll make a little fuss. *Hooray!*" said Lizzie.

"*Hooray* yourself." Penny flopped down on the bed. "When I was six, all we had at my party were dumb balloons. You are getting balloons and special prizes at your party. I'll have to help, just like always. It is no fun being the big sister!"

"Don't you want to know what I want for my birthday?" Lizzie yelled. "I want a two-wheeler. I want a skateboard like Jenny's. I want a horse."

"Could you please not yell," said Penny. "Doesn't anyone want to know what I want for my birthday?"

"Not really."

"Well, I am going to tell you anyway," said Penny. "I want a big sister. I'm tired of being the grown-up one."

"But then you won't be the boss anymore," Lizzie said.

"Being the boss isn't everything," said Penny. "If I fall, I am not supposed to cry. If you fall, you can cry. Everyone feels sorry for you.

"If I want to sit on Daddy's lap, he tells me I am getting too big. If you want to sit on Daddy's lap, you climb up and go to sleep. It's not fair."

"What's the matter?" asked Lizzie.

"Nothing is the matter."

"Don't you want to do the dinosaur puzzle?" Lizzie asked.

"Not really," Penny said.

"What do you want to do then?"

"I want to be the little sister!"

"Okay," said Lizzie. "I'll be the big sister."

"Hah!"

"I will. I know how," said Lizzie.

"Okay, smarty, we will see how you like it. Let's do the dinosaur puzzle."

Lizzie yelled, "Why are you dropping the pieces all over?"

"That is what little sisters do with puzzles," Penny told her. "You have to pick them up. You are the big sister."

While Lizzie was looking for the pieces, Penny said, "I will get some juice."

"Help!" Penny yelled. "I spilled it." Lizzie ran to get a rag.

"My shirt is all wet," Penny yelled. "I need a clean one." Lizzie brought a shirt.

"Clean me up first," Penny told her. "I am all sticky." Lizzie cleaned Penny up. "Help me put my shirt on," Penny said.

"Can't you do anything?" Lizzie asked.

"Well," Penny said. "How do you like being the big sister so far?"

"It's not so bad," answered Lizzie.

"Okay, then. Let's jump rope," Penny said. *Whoosh-thump. Whoosh-thump.*

"What's the matter? Why are you jumping like that?" asked Lizzie. "You are going to fall."

"That is how little sisters jump," Penny said. "If I fall, you will have to pick me up. You are the big sister."

Kerthunk. "Help!" yelled Penny. "My knee is really bleeding! It hurts!"

"Yick!" Lizzie said. She ran away.

"I should have known!" yelled Penny. "You don't know how to be the big sister. You are just a baby."

Penny looked down at her knee. She cried and cried and cried. "At least when you are the little sister, you can cry as much as you want," Penny thought. Then she felt better.

Lizzie came back pulling a wagon. "Get in," she said. She pulled Penny to her room.

"Lie down," Lizzie said. She tucked Penny into bed. "I will be right back with your medicine."

"I don't want any medicine!" Penny shouted.

"You must have this medicine," Lizzie said when she came back. The wagon was filled with Lizzie's very own stuffed snake, Peter, her favorite King Kong picture, and a big orange. "See," Lizzie said. "I *can* be the big sister."

"You are a pretty good big sister after all." Penny hugged her sister.

"You are a pretty good big sister, too," said Lizzie.

"Thank you for giving me the *best* birthday present," said Penny. "Don't forget. Next week I will be *eight*. I can go to bed later than you. I will be very grown up. After all, I'm the *big* sister."

1. What did Lizzie and Penny decide about being a big sister?
2. Why did Penny want to be the little sister?
3. Why did Lizzie try to act like a big sister?
4. What made Penny think that being a little sister was better?
5. When in the story did you begin to think that Penny was tired of playing the little sister?

Think and Write

Suppose a child were asked to be the boss of your classroom. Write a story that tells what things that child would need to do.

Brother

by Mary Ann Hoberman

I had a little brother
And I brought him to my mother
And I said I want another
Little brother for a change.
But she said don't be a bother
So I took him to my father
And I said this little bother
Of a brother's very strange.
But he said one little brother
Is exactly like another
And every little brother
Misbehaves a bit he said.
So I took the little bother
From my mother and my father
And I put the little bother
Of a brother back to bed.

Jamie has some special homework. What is Jamie supposed to do? How does he do it?

The Galumpagalooses

by Eloise Jarvis McGraw

Jamie was given something special to do after school one day. His teacher, Ms. Morris, asked him to draw something no one had ever seen before. Jamie was excited, but he wasn't sure how to do this. When he got home, he told his mother what he was supposed to do. She told him to ask their friend, Mr. Rollo, for help. Mr. Rollo was an artist who lived in the same building as Jamie.

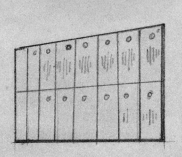

Jamie went to Mr. Rollo's door and knocked. Mr. Rollo opened the door. "Hi there, Jamie. How's it going?" asked Mr. Rollo.

"Mr. Rollo, you're an artist, aren't you?" asked Jamie.

"That's a fact," answered Mr. Rollo. "I'm certainly not anything else."

"A real artist?" asked Jamie.

"That's a different question," Mr. Rollo said, as he looked down at Jamie.

"Can you draw a picture of something that nobody's ever seen before?"

Mr. Rollo blinked and then said, "Certainly, I do that all the time."

"Really?" Jamie asked. He was excited. "You said that you only drew pictures of furniture and TV sets and . . ."

143

"That's at work. At home I draw things nobody's ever seen before." Mr. Rollo smiled at Jamie and said, "Come on in and see."

Jamie had never been in Mr. Rollo's home before. It wasn't what he expected. Mostly it was one long room, with some furniture way back in a corner and a strong smell of paint. There were pictures all over the walls. Jamie just stood and stared at the pictures—first one, then the next, then the next. All of the pictures were of things nobody had ever seen before.

"What are they, Mr. Rollo?" Jamie asked at last. "What do you call them?"

"Sometimes I call them abstractions. Sometimes I just call them shapes. Now and then I call one a galumpagaloos," Mr. Rollo answered.

Jamie laughed. He knew Mr. Rollo was joking. "But how do you draw an abstraction, or a galumpagaloos? How do you start?" he asked.

Mr. Rollo thought a minute, then said, "I look at something."

"Oh," said Jamie, not sure if that would help. "But it's supposed to be something nobody's ever seen."

"Nobody ever *has* seen it the way I see it, because nobody else is me. Look there, Jamie," said Mr. Rollo, turning Jamie to face a big painting on the wall. "Did you ever see the thing in that picture before?"

Jamie looked carefully. "No."

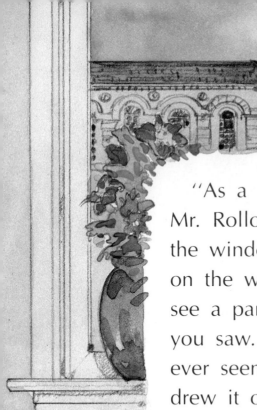

"As a matter of fact, you have," said
Mr. Rollo. He turned Jamie to face
the window. There was a bowl of flowers
on the windowsill. Outside, Jamie could
see a part of the library. "That's what
you saw. I saw something nobody had
ever seen before—not even me, until I
drew it on the paper."

Jamie stared at the big painting,
then at the window, and then at the big
painting again. Slowly he began to
understand. He felt very excited.
He asked, "Could I draw one of those
galumpagalooses, do you think?"

"I expect you could," said Mr. Rollo.
"You'll never know till you try."

So Jamie tried. He hurried home and
found some paper and a pencil. Then he
looked at things. He looked until he
really saw them in his very own way, and
then he drew.

Right away he knew he was drawing things he'd never seen before, until he saw them on his paper. By the time his mother came to look, Jamie had three sheets of paper covered with drawings. When he showed them to her, she said she'd certainly never seen such things. Jamie wasn't sure what Ms. Morris would say, though.

The next morning at school, he took all his pictures to Ms. Morris's desk. She looked at him and then at the papers in his hand. He handed her one of his pictures. "Did you ever see that thing before?"

Ms. Morris looked at it carefully. Then she said, "No."

Jamie began to smile, because he knew she had, but not the way he had seen it. "It's a galumpagaloos," he said. He handed her his other drawings. "Here are eight more galumpagalooses."

Jamie watched Ms. Morris spread them out on her desk and stare at them, first one, then the next, then the next. Finally she looked up and said, "You did it."

"I told you I could do it," said Jamie. They grinned at each other.

1. Why did Jamie's mother tell him to go to Mr. Rollo?

2. How did Mr. Rollo help Jamie?

3. What is an abstraction?

4. What did you think about Mr. Rollo's name for shapes or abstractions? Why?

5. When in the story did you first think Jamie would make Ms. Morris happy with his work?

Think and Write

Find something and look at it very closely. Draw a picture or an abstraction of it. Then write a sentence that tells what your picture is about and where you saw what you drew.

*In "The Galumpagalooses,"
Jamie drew things in his very
own way. Read to find out what
makes the art of Henri Matisse
so special.*

Henri Matisse, Artist

by Ruth Michaels

What would you think if you saw a
grown man cutting things out of
colored paper? Would you guess that
this man was a famous artist? Well, he
was. The man was Henri Matisse.

The Early Years

Henri Matisse was born in France in 1869. As a child, he didn't show any real interest in art. He studied law when he was a young man. Then one day, when he was sick, his mother brought him a box of paints to help him pass the time until he felt better.

Matisse started to paint by making copies of famous paintings. He soon found that he liked to paint so much that he wanted to become an artist. He decided to go to school and study art. He also went to famous museums to look at the paintings of other artists.

Matisse said, "For some time I painted just like anyone else. But things didn't go well at all, and I was unhappy. Then, little by little, I began to paint as I felt."

The Later Years

Matisse always kept trying new things. His art was most different from that of other artists because of the way he used colors and shapes. Matisse said that when he wanted to paint a picture of fall, he did not try to copy just what he saw. Instead he painted the way fall made him feel. Matisse never painted sad things, because he wanted his art to make people feel happy.

Matisse became a very famous artist. People began to buy more and more of his paintings.

When Matisse was over seventy years old, he started using scissors and colored paper for his art. He cut out shapes and pasted these shapes on another piece of paper. Matisse called this "drawing with scissors." In the last four years of his life, Matisse did only cut-outs. He was not well, and this was the only work he could do. He didn't mind, though. When he was drawing with scissors, he said he was "cutting the colors out alive."

Matisse said that an artist has to look at life through the eyes of a child. By this he meant that an artist has to look at everything as if that artist were seeing it for the first time.

To some people, Matisse's artwork might seem like the work of a child. In fact, it could only have been done by a great artist. Today Matisse's paintings and his cut-outs are in museums all over the world.

1. How did Henri Matisse make people happy?

2. How did Matisse use scissors to make art?

3. How was Matisse's art different from the art of others?

4. Do you like Matisse's art? Why or why not?

5. What did you read on page 153 that made you think that people liked Matisse's art?

Matisse drew a picture showing how fall made him feel. Think about how fall makes you feel. Write a paragraph that tells what you can see and hear and that shows how fall makes you feel.

Alphabetical Order

Look at the names *Clark* and *Brown*. Which one would you find first in a telephone book? Why? Did you say *Brown* because the letter *B* comes before the letter *C* in the alphabet? Telephone books list names in **alphabetical order**, or in the order of the letters of the alphabet.

Now look at the names *Suter* and *Sweet*. Which one of these would come first in a telephone book? Because the first letter of each name is the letter *S*, you have to look at the second letter of each name. The second letter of *Suter* is *u*. The second letter of *Sweet* is *w*. The letter *u* comes before the letter *w* in the alphabet, so the name *Suter* would come before *Sweet* in the telephone book.

Now look at the names *Waxman* and *Walsh*. Which one of these names would come first? Notice that the first two letters of each name are the same. You must look at the third letter. The third letter in *Waxman* is *x*. The third letter in *Walsh* is *l*. Because the letter *l* comes before *x* in the alphabet, the name *Walsh* would come before the name *Waxman* in the telephone book.

Names are listed in alphabetical order in a telephone book. Words in a dictionary are also listed in alphabetical order. When you want to find something in one of these books, you have to look at the letters in the names or words. Remember, when words have the same first letter, look at the second letter of each word. When words have the same first and second letters, look at the third letter of each word. Knowing about alphabetical order will help you use a telephone book and a dictionary.

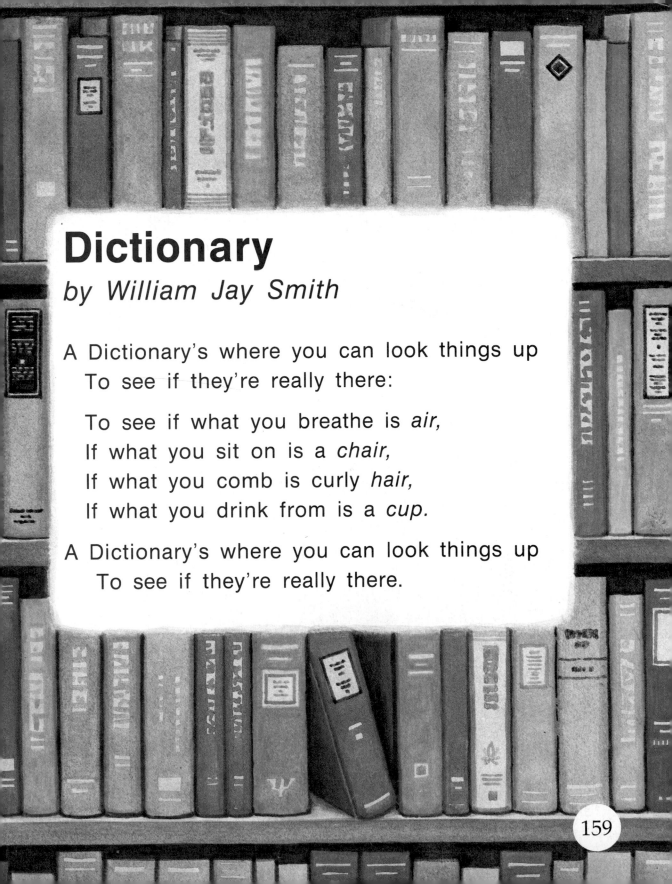

Dictionary

by William Jay Smith

A Dictionary's where you can look things up
  To see if they're really there:

  To see if what you breathe is *air,*
  If what you sit on is a *chair,*
  If what you comb is curly *hair,*
  If what you drink from is a *cup.*

A Dictionary's where you can look things up
  To see if they're really there.

The Mystery of Sara Beth

by Polly Putnam

The mystery began in December. Becky
and her friends were working. Wind and
snow blew hard on the windows. The door
opened, and a girl walked in and stood
near the door. She wore a furry blue coat.

Miss Harris, the teacher, spoke to
her. Then she said, "Class, this is our
new girl. Her name is Sara Beth." Miss
Harris pointed to the desk in front of
Becky. "Sit there, Sara Beth."

Becky smiled when Sara Beth sat down, but Sara Beth didn't smile back. Sara Beth didn't turn around all morning. At noon Becky took Sara Beth to lunch. "Will you eat with us?" Becky asked. Sara Beth shook her head and went to a table by herself.

Becky and her friends sat at a table together. They talked about Sara Beth. "Why doesn't she want to make friends?" asked Becky.

"Maybe she is shy," said David.

"If we're nice to her, she'll soon be our friend," said Janie.

Becky, David, and Janie helped Sara Beth. Becky found some books for her. She gave Sara Beth a pencil and a ruler.

Sara Beth said, "Thank you," but she didn't smile, and she didn't talk any more.

161

Janie took Sara Beth to the gym. She
told Sara Beth the rules for the games.
Sara Beth said, "Thank you," but she
didn't say anything else.

David showed Sara Beth the library. He
helped Sara Beth take out a book. Sara
Beth said, "Thank you," but that was all.

"I give up," said Janie after a few days.
"Sara Beth doesn't want any friends."

"I want to know why," said Becky.
"Everyone wants friends."

Becky wanted to solve the mystery of why Sara Beth didn't want friends. She looked for clues.

Becky saw that Sara Beth's blue jeans were old and faded, but many children wore faded jeans. No, Sara Beth's clothes were not a clue to the mystery.

Becky had another idea. Maybe Sara Beth was afraid she couldn't do her schoolwork. Becky peeked at Sara Beth's papers. They said *Good* and had only a few red marks on them. Sara Beth often raised her hand to answer questions. She was on the same spelling page as Becky. No, Sara Beth wasn't worried about her schoolwork. Becky couldn't guess what was making Sara Beth so unfriendly.

Sara Beth stayed alone until the day Miss Harris put a big cage on the table. The children came up to the table and saw two guinea pigs. The children named the guinea pigs Harriet and Smitty.

"Someone will have to help feed and care for the guinea pigs every day," said Miss Harris. "Mondays and Thursdays the cage will have to be cleaned."

"I'll help," said Sara Beth. "I'll do it every Monday."

The next Monday Sara Beth cleaned the cage. She put down clean newspapers and hay. She filled the water bottle with fresh water, and she set out new food.

Then Sara Beth let Harriet and Smitty play on the table. She picked up Smitty and held him close while she petted him.

Becky was more puzzled than ever. Why would Sara Beth make friends with animals and not with her classmates?

During the next few days, three strange things happened. They gave Becky the clues she needed.

The first strange thing happened in the coatroom after school. Becky was alone with Sara Beth. A reading book dropped to the floor. Sara Beth had hidden it under her coat.

Becky said, "You know Miss Harris doesn't let us take reading books home. She's afraid they will be lost."

Sara Beth's face turned red. "Please don't tell," she said. Becky didn't tell, but she had her first clue.

The second strange thing happened during George's birthday party in school. He gave everyone a glass of punch and an apple. Sara Beth drank her punch, but she didn't eat her apple. She put it in her desk.

The third strange thing happened on a Thursday. It was Janie's day to clean the guinea pig cage. While Janie was cleaning the cage, Harriet jumped off the table. She ran all around under the desks. All the children tried to catch her. Everyone was laughing and shouting.

Becky was the only one watching Sara Beth. Sara Beth wasn't chasing Harriet. Sara Beth was standing on a chair. Her face was white, and she was shaking. She was afraid! Becky had her third clue. It was the strangest of all.

Becky thought about the three clues.

1. Sara Beth broke the rule about taking a reading book home.
2. Sara Beth saved her apple instead of eating it.
3. Sometimes Sara Beth loved guinea pigs, and sometimes she was afraid of them.

All at once Becky solved the mystery! She knew why Sara Beth would not make any friends.

Becky could hardly wait for the chance to see Sara Beth alone. During art Miss Harris said, "Becky and Sara Beth, please go to the art room to get more paint."

In the art room, Sara Beth reached for a jar of paint. "Tell me," said Becky. "Are you Sara, or are you Beth?"

Sara Beth almost dropped the paint. "What do you mean?" she asked.

"I know you're a twin," said Becky, "and I know you take turns coming to school."

Sara Beth's eyes opened wide. "It's true," she said. "How did you know?"

Becky said, "You gave me some clues. I guessed that the reading book and the apple were going home to someone. I didn't know who until today, when you jumped up in the chair. You are afraid of Harriet. Your twin is not."

Sara Beth sat down. "I'm Beth," she said. "Now I have given away the secret." Beth put her head in her hands. Becky put her arm around Beth.

"You were both unfriendly so no one would find out your secret," said Becky.

"Yes," said Beth.

"I don't understand," said Becky. "Why couldn't you both come to school?"

"We have just moved from a place where the weather is not so cold," said Beth. "We have only one warm coat. Sara and I take turns wearing it."

Becky said, "After school we'll tell Miss Harris. She'll know what to do."

"I'm afraid she'll be angry," said Beth.

Miss Harris wasn't angry. "We'll look in the office, Beth," she said. "There are extra hats. Maybe there is an extra coat."

Beth looked surprised. "You mean there are other children without warm clothes?" she asked.

Miss Harris smiled. "Certainly."

The next day two smiling girls walked into Becky's classroom. One was wearing a furry blue coat. The other was wearing a brown coat.

Now Becky had a new mystery to solve. Which twin was Sara, and which was Beth?

1. What was the mystery of Sara Beth?

2. Why didn't both twins go to school?

3. What three clues did Becky use to solve the mystery?

4. Do you think Sara and Beth had a good plan for going to school? Why do you think that?

5. When in the story did you know that Becky was sure there was a mystery about Sara Beth?

Think and Write

Pretend you have a twin. Write a paragraph about how your life might be different. If you are a twin, write about what it would be like not to be a twin.

Character

All stories and plays have characters. Characters are the people or the animals in a story. In "The Galumpagalooses," the characters are Jamie, Jamie's mother, Mr. Rollo, and Ms. Morris.

Some story characters are more important than others. The more important characters are called the **major** characters. Jamie is the major character in "The Galumpagalooses."

Other characters are not as important as the major character. These are the **minor** characters. Mr. Rollo, Jamie's mother, and Ms. Morris are the minor characters in "The Galumpagalooses."

Read the paragraph below. Who is the major character? Who are the minor characters? How do you know?

Karen was so sad that she cried. Her best friend, Margie, was moving away. Karen and Margie had lived next door to each other for a long time. Karen's mother and father were also sad, but they didn't say much. Karen wondered why they were so quiet.

Karen is the major character. We are told how she feels and what she does. Karen's mother and father and Margie are minor characters. We are not told very much about them.

When you read, decide who the major and minor characters are. Remember, major characters are the most important people or animals in the story. Minor characters are not as important.

You don't always need words to talk. What are some ways you can talk without words?

Talking Without Words

Story and pictures by Marie Hall Ets

"Give me some of your peanuts," says Bear, but he doesn't say it in words. He just opens his mouth and holds up his paw.

"I want to see *them* without their seeing *me*," says Sister, but not in words. She just hides behind the house and peeks.

"I love the smell of flowers!" says Little Brother, but he doesn't say it in words. He just runs and smells the flowers whenever he sees some.

"Come here. I have something nice for you," says Mother to Little Brother, but not in words. She just motions to him.

When I'm too hot, I take off my coat. When Sister's too cold, she hugs herself and shivers. We don't need to use words to say so.

"Throw it to me, too!" says Little Brother
when Big Brother and Sister are playing
ball. He just says it with his hands.

"I don't want to hear!" says Little
Brother when Mother starts scolding. He
doesn't say it in words. He just covers
his ears.

"Don't wake the baby," says Mother, but without using words. She just motions by putting a finger on her lips and Little Brother understands.

"Good-bye!" I wave as you go away. You are too far for words, so I only hope you'll turn around and wave good-bye to me.

1. How can you talk without words?

2. What animal made people know, without using words, what it wanted? How did that animal do it?

3. Tell four things people said. How did they say them without words?

4. Which of the ways of talking without words do you use most?

5. When was it easiest for you to tell what was being said from looking at the picture?

Think about something you could say without words. Draw a picture to show how you could say it. Then write a sentence saying it in words.

179

Sammy and Jacob are good friends. How do they help each other?

My Friend Jacob

by *Lucille Clifton*

My best friend lives next door. His name is Jacob. He is my very, very best friend.

We do things together, Jacob and me. We love to play basketball together. Jacob always makes a basket on the first try. He helps me to learn how to hold the ball so that I can make baskets, too.

My mother used to say, "Be careful with Jacob and that ball. He might hurt you." Now she knows that Jacob wouldn't hurt anybody, especially his very, very best friend.

I love to sit on the steps for hours and watch the cars go by with Jacob. He knows the name of every kind of car. Even if he only sees it just for a minute, Jacob can tell you the kind of car.

Jacob is helping me learn to name the cars, too. When I make a mistake, Jacob never ever laughs. He just says, "No, no, Sam. Try again." Then I do. He is my best, best friend.

When I have to go to the store, Jacob goes with me to help. His mother used to say, "You don't have to have Jacob tagging along with you like that, Sammy." Now she knows we like to go to the store together. Jacob helps me to carry, and I help Jacob to remember.

"Red is for stop," I say if Jacob forgets. "Green is for go."

"Thank you, Sam," Jacob always says.

Jacob's birthday and my birthday are two days apart. Sometimes we celebrate together. Last year he made me a surprise. He had been having a secret for weeks and weeks, and my mother knew, and his mother knew, but they wouldn't tell me.

Jacob would stay in his house for an hour every afternoon and not say anything to me when he came out. He would just smile and smile.

On my birthday, my mother made a cake especially for me with eight candles. Jacob's mother made a cake especially for him with seventeen candles. We sat on the porch and sang and blew out our candles. Jacob blew out all seventeen candles in one breath because he's bigger.

Then my mother smiled, and Jacob's mother smiled and said, "Give it to him, Jacob dear." My friend Jacob smiled and handed me a card.

HAPPY BIRTHDAY SAM
JACOB

He had printed it all by himself! All by himself, he printed my name and everything! It was neat!

My very best friend Jacob does so much to help me, I wanted to help him, too. One day I decided to teach him how to knock before he comes into my house.

Jacob would just walk into people's houses if he knew them. If he didn't know them, he would stand on the porch until somebody noticed him and let him in. "I wish Jacob would knock on the door," I heard my mother say.

I decided to help him learn. Every day I would tell Jacob, but he would always forget. He would just open the door and walk right in. My mother said maybe it was too hard for him and I shouldn't worry about it. I felt bad because Jacob always helped me so much, and I wanted to be able to help him, too.

I kept telling him and he kept forgetting, so one day I just said, "Never mind, Jacob, maybe it is too hard."

"What's the matter, Sam?" Jacob asked me.

"Never mind, Jacob," was all I said.

Next day we were sitting in our dining room when my mother and my father and I heard this really loud knocking at the door. Then the door popped open and Jacob stuck his head in. "I'm knocking, Sam!" he yelled.

Boy, I jumped right up from the table, and grinned and hugged Jacob. He grinned and hugged me, too. He is my very, very, very best friend in the whole wide world!

1. How did Sammy and Jacob help each other?

2. How did Sammy feel about Jacob?

3. What special thing did Jacob do for Sammy?

4. How did you feel when Jacob knocked on Sammy's door? Why?

5. What did you read on page 181 that told you that Jacob could learn things?

Think about how Sammy and Jacob helped each other. Pretend you are Sammy. Write a paragraph that tells things you might teach Jacob and things Jacob might teach you.

Thinking About "Bridges"

In this unit, you learned that people have different ways of building bridges to others. Sometimes a bridge is built when two people try to understand each other.

Penny and Lizzie traded places and built a bridge of understanding. Mr. Rollo helped Jamie to see things in a new way. Matisse reached out with his paintings and cut-outs.

Sara and Beth needed the bridge of friendship and found it with Becky and their classmates. Jacob and Sam had a special bridge between them.

As you read other stories, think about the problems people have when there is no bridge of understanding. Then think about the bridges that people build to reach each other.

1. In what ways are the stories "Little Boss" and "The Mystery of Sara Beth" the same? How are they different?

2. Do you think that Mr. Rollo from "The Galumpagalooses" would have liked to meet Matisse? Why?

3. How are Jamie from "The Galumpagalooses" and Sammy and Jacob alike? How are they different?

4. Which person in this unit do you think did the best job of building a bridge of understanding? Why?

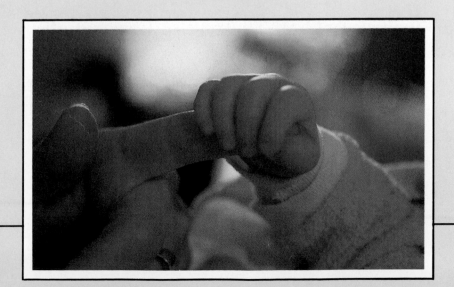

Read on Your Own

Poinsettia and Her Family by Felicia Bond.
  Harper. Poinsettia Pig thinks her house
  would be perfect without her noisy,
  always-in-the-way brothers and sisters.

Horrible Hannah by Barbara Bottner. Crown.
  Two girls see a sign in the neighbor's
  yard and think the neighbor is horrible.
  They have made a horrible mistake.

The Boy Who Didn't Believe in Spring by
  Lucille Clifton. Dutton. A boy who
  lives in the city doesn't believe in
  spring. He decides to go out and look
  for it.

Ed Emberley's Great Thumbprint Drawing Book
  by Ed Emberley. Little, Brown. Learn
  how to make things using thumbprints
  and a few lines. Some of the things you
  can make are bugs, birds, fish, and
  people.

Gilberto and the Wind by Marie Hall Ets. Viking. A boy talks about all the things the wind can do.

A House Is a House for Me by Mary Ann Hoberman. Viking. This book tells about the many places where people, animals, and things can live.

Let's Make Rabbits by Leo Lionni. Pantheon. A pair of scissors and a pencil decide to make rabbits. Then the make-believe rabbits eat a real carrot.

Meet Matisse by Nelly Munthe. Little, Brown. This book tells how Henri Matisse made his cut-outs and how you can try it.

Making Things: The Hand Book of Creative Discovery by Ann Wiseman. Little, Brown. This book tells you how to make things such as puppets, candles, and toys.

Unit 4

Patterns

A pattern is something that is repeated over and over again. In this unit you will read stories that have been told over and over again. These stories were first told long ago.

Other stories will help you to know the pattern of life in the past. One story is from a book that children have been reading for many, many years. Your parents or grandparents may have read this story when they were young.

As you read, think about why these stories are in a unit called "Patterns."

This is an old tale that has been told over and over again. What does Country Mouse learn from his visit to the city?

City Mouse and Country Mouse

An Aesop fable retold by Jane Lawrence

Once, in a field of tall grass, there lived a small mouse. He was quite happy with his life, all in all. He had a snug place to sleep where he was safe. He had plenty of food to eat, too. From here and there he picked up crumbs and vegetables. On good days he might even find some dry cheese.

Yes, indeed. Country Mouse had a good life and was very happy.

One day, as he leaned back on a
small pile of grass, he wondered
whatever had happened to his cousin,
City Mouse. He wrote a letter asking
City Mouse how he was and if he'd like
to come for a visit to the country.

For a long time Country Mouse didn't
hear anything from his cousin. He
almost forgot about the letter. Then one
day, who should turn up in his field
but his cousin, City Mouse.

The two mice were very glad to see
each other. They talked and talked all
afternoon about this and that, catching
up on all the news.

For dinner Country Mouse went out to get all the best bits of food he could find. He wanted to serve an extra-nice meal on this happy day.

As City Mouse was wiping his mouth after dinner, he said, "Well, that was not bad, cousin. It was not bad, but not good either. How can you stand to live this way?"

"What do you mean?" asked Country Mouse. "Live what way?"

City Mouse sniffed, and smoothed his whiskers with great care. "Well," he said, "it's just so dull here. There is nothing to do, no one to see, no place to go. I can't believe your food! What can I say?"

"What's wrong with my food?" asked Country Mouse, his feelings hurt. After all, he had worked very hard to fix a good dinner. "Didn't you get plenty to eat?"

"Oh, I got plenty," said City Mouse. "But, cousin, it was not my idea of good. It was plain and dull."

Country Mouse's face grew sad. "I'm sorry you didn't like it," he said, trying not to let his hurt feelings show.

"I guess there isn't anything you can do about it," said City Mouse. "Out here in the country, you just don't have much to pick from."

"I did the very best I could," said Country Mouse in a small voice.

"Of course you did," said City Mouse. "Now, I have a great idea. You can come back to the city with me. There are things to do, places to go. Wait until you taste the food I will serve!"

The two cousins set off for the city. Soon they were at City Mouse's house. It was everything City Mouse had said it would be.

The rugs were beautiful bright colors. In each room were beautiful chairs and tables and lights. Best of all was the kitchen. Country Mouse ran up and down everywhere. Everything in the kitchen was shining and bright. There, right in front of his eyes, was a mountain of food.

Never in his whole life had he seen such food. "May I have some of it?" Country Mouse asked City Mouse.

"Of course you may," answered City Mouse. "What do you think I've been telling you? This is the best place in the whole world to live."

So Country Mouse ate and ate. He had never eaten such food. He thought he might never be so happy again. "The city is the place for me," he said. "Do you eat like this every day?"

"But of course!" said City Mouse. "This is the city! We live very well here." City Mouse sniffed, and smoothed his whiskers, the way he did when he was pleased with himself.

Just then came a loud banging and thumping noise down the hall. Country Mouse was just getting ready to take one more large bite of cheese, but he stopped cold.

"What is that?" he asked, and looked over at City Mouse.

199

"Tell you later," City Mouse panted.
He grabbed Country Mouse's paw and
pulled him hard. "Run for your life!"

They ran, slipping and sliding, as
the noise got closer and closer. At
last they were safe behind some cups
on a high shelf. Country Mouse took a
deep breath.

"What was that all about?" he asked.

"It was the house animals," answered
City Mouse. "When they come into the
kitchen, we have to run, or they'll get
us."

"Is it like this every day?" asked
Country Mouse.

"Every day," answered City Mouse. "You get used to it after a while, though."

"Not me," said Country Mouse. "I don't want to get used to it." As soon as the house animals went away, Country Mouse jumped down and headed for the kitchen door.

"Where are you going?" shouted City Mouse. "I have much more to show you!"

"Not me," said Country Mouse over his shoulder. "I don't need to see anything else. I'm going back to the country right now."

"But there isn't anything to do there," said City Mouse. "You'll never eat the way you ate here tonight."

"Maybe I won't," said Country Mouse. "On the other hand, I'll never be eaten either, and I don't have to be afraid. I can eat my plain food without having to worry about someone coming to get me. So long, City Mouse. I hope I can see you again some day. Come visit me again, if you are able."

Country Mouse ran all the way back to his home in the country as fast as his little legs would carry him. He lived a long and happy life, even if he didn't have such an exciting life.

Remember: Be happy with what you have.

1. What did Country Mouse learn?

2. Why did City Mouse ask Country Mouse to come to the city?

3. Why did Country Mouse run away from the city?

4. How do you feel about Country Mouse returning to the country? What else could he have done?

5. When in the story did you first think that Country Mouse might not want to stay in the city?

Think and Write

Pretend you are either City Mouse or Country Mouse. Write a paragraph that tells three things you like about where you live.

The boy in this story has one grandfather who lives in the city and one who lives in the country. What does the boy learn from each grandfather?

City Grandfather, Country Grandfather

by Robert Hasselblad

I have two grandfathers. One lives in the city. One lives in the country.

My city grandfather lives on a wide street, lined with houses. In front of his house are a sidewalk, a streetlight, and a small yard.

My country grandfather lives at the end of a dirt road. In front of his house are a large gate, an apple tree, and a big yard.

My city grandfather works in an office.
He rides up to his office in an elevator.
He is a businessman.

My country grandfather works in his
fields and barn. He rides on a big green
tractor. He is a farmer.

My city grandfather has a big desk with
a telephone on it. He talks to many people
on the telephone every day. He also has
an adding machine in his office. He adds
lots of numbers on it. The answers come
out on a long roll of paper.

My country grandfather has many cows
that he milks each day. He has machines
that do this. He stores the milk until a
truck comes to collect it.

When I visit my city grandfather at his office, he lets me add numbers on the adding machine. I lick stamps for his letters. We take the mail to the mail drop near the elevator. He tells me that I am learning about business.

When I visit my country grandfather, he lets me pet the cows to keep them happy. He lets me ride with him on the tractor. We go to the mailbox at the end of the road. He tells me that I am learning about farming.

My city grandfather drives a shiny blue car. Sometimes he drives to other cities on business.

My country grandfather drives an old red truck. Sometimes he drives to town to get things he needs.

When I visit my city grandfather, we ride our bikes together all around town. We buy popcorn to feed the birds in the park.

When I visit my country grandfather, we build a fire. Then we sing songs.

At the end of every visit, both my city grandfather and my country grandfather do exactly the same thing. They both give me big bear hugs and say, "See you real soon!" Maybe when I grow up, I'll be a farmer and live in the country. Maybe I'll be a businessman and live in the city. I know about both.

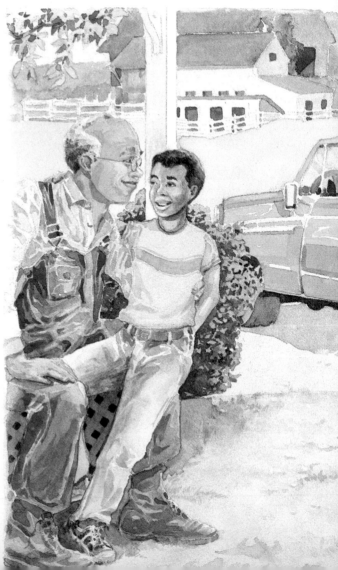

1. Tell three things the boy does with his city grandfather.

2. Tell three things the boy does with his country grandfather.

3. What two things do the grandfathers say the boy is learning?

4. What did you like best about each grandfather? Why?

5. Find the words that tell how the grandfathers feel about the boy.

Think

and

Write

Pretend you are going to visit one of the grandfathers. Write a story telling which grandfather you would like to visit and why. Tell what you would like to do during your visit.

Rudolph Is Tired of the City

by Gwendolyn Brooks

These buildings are too close to me.
I'd like to *push* away.
I'd like to live in the country,
And spread my arms all day.

I'd like to spread my breath out, too—
As farmers' sons and daughters do.

I'd tend the cows and chickens.
I'd do the other chores.
Then, all the hours left I'd go
A-spreading out-of-doors.

Comparisons

Look at the picture below. Can you find four ways these people are the same?

Did you find the four ways the people are the same? Did you say that they are both boys? Did you see that both have black hair? Did you see that both are dressed the same? Did you see that both are playing music? When you think about how things are the same, you **compare** them.

How could you compare City Mouse and Country Mouse? Did you remember that they were both mice? Did you say that they were both afraid of the house animals? Did you remember that they both liked good food?

Now read this paragraph. How does the writer compare the girls?

Susan and Donna both like to ice skate. Both girls got new skates as birthday presents. In the wintertime, they skate every weekend. Susan is learning to do tricks on her skates. Donna is learning to do tricks, too.

Did you find four ways that the writer compared Susan and Donna?

As you read, remember to think about how the writer compares people and things. Remember that when you compare, you tell how people or things or places are the same. Understanding how things are the same is one way of finding meaning as you read.

Housekeeping

by George E. Coon

Mom called Sis the neatest kid
For cleaning her room the way she did,
But Sis is shorter and nearer the floor,
So she can see the messes more.

My books and clothes were sort of scattered,
But I could find the ones that mattered.
To hear Mom talk, you'd certainly think
That everything's there but the kitchen sink.

I'll clean up my room,
   'Cause I can't escape.
And I'll spend next week
   Getting it back in shape.

Like "Country Mouse and City Mouse," this is an old tale. What does the ant in this story teach the grasshopper?

The Ant and the Grasshopper

An Aesop fable retold by M. Drummond

It was summertime. Every day the grasshopper fiddled and sang. He didn't worry about anything at all. He loved the excitement of summer.

Every day the ant worked very hard gathering food. Then he carried it to a safe place.

"Why do you work so hard?" the grasshopper asked the ant.

"I work because winter is coming," said the ant.

"Winter is a long way off," said the grasshopper. "Come and dance."

"I can't," said the ant. "I told you, winter is coming."

"Well, it is summer now," said the grasshopper. "Now is the time to fiddle and sing. Feel that nice hot sun. Look at the nice green grass. Smell the beautiful flowers."

The ant sighed. "I'd like to dance and fiddle and sing with you," he said. "Perhaps when my work is done I can."

At that the grasshopper laughed. "You'll never be done. You just run around gathering food and carrying it from one place to the other all day. You miss all the excitement in life."

The ant gave a small smile. "I know it may seem that I am missing the excitement, but wait and see. When winter comes, I'll be thankful that I worked so hard."

"Well, that's not the life for me," said the grasshopper. "I can't think about winter now. When it gets here, I'll think about it."

All summer long it was the same. Every day the grasshopper fiddled and sang. Every day the grasshopper tried to talk the ant into singing and dancing with him. Every day the ant said he didn't have time. Every day the ant worked harder and harder, gathering and storing up food.

Then the days began to change. The leaves on the trees turned different colors. The flowers began to dry up. Pretty soon cold winds began to blow, and the sun was not so warm in the daytime. The nights got colder and colder, and snow began to fall.

The ant kept warm in his anthill. When he was hungry, he ate the food he had stored up from the summer.

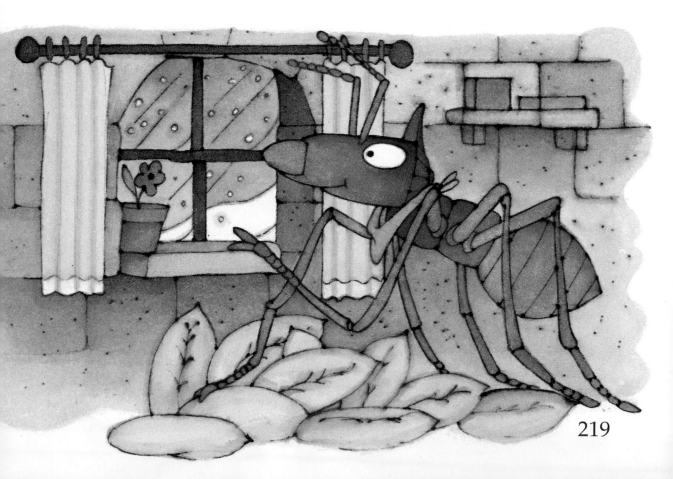

The grasshopper hopped all over looking for something to eat. There was nothing to be found anywhere. He got thinner and thinner. He was very tired, he was very cold, and he was very hungry.

At last the grasshopper knew he could not last another day. He went to the ant and said, "Please give me some food. Just a bite would be nice. I am so very hungry. I can't find anything to eat, and you have so much."

"I'm very sorry," said the ant, for he was a kind ant. "I really wish I could help you, but I can't. I have only enough food for myself and my family."

"I shouldn't have played and sung all summer," sighed the grasshopper. "I should have gathered and stored up food the way you did." The grasshopper pulled his wings close around him and walked sadly away into the wind and cold.

The hardworking ant could have said, "I told you so." He was a kind ant, though, so he didn't say anything at all. He just shook his head and watched the grasshopper walk away.

Remember: Save while you can. You may not have a chance later.

1. What did the ant teach the grasshopper?

2. Why didn't the ant share his food with the grasshopper? How did you feel about this?

3. Why did the ant work hard all summer?

4. Where in the story did you learn that the grasshopper never worked?

Think and Write

Think about how the ant and the grasshopper are alike. For example, they are both insects. Write a paragraph that tells two more ways the ant and the grasshopper are alike.

Did you know that there is more than one kind of squirrel? Read to find out how the gray squirrel and the ground squirrel are the same. How are they different?

Squirrels in Winter

by Ruth Michaels

Gray Squirrel

The gray squirrel is hungry. It comes down from its nest high up in a tree to look for food. As the squirrel runs along the ground, it sees a flower. The flower looks very good, so the squirrel stops to have a bite to eat. The squirrel turns the flower in its paws as it takes small bites. A flower isn't what the squirrel really wants, though.

The gray squirrel is really searching for nuts. That's what the gray squirrel likes best of all. It finds a nut. The nut tastes very good. The squirrel holds the nut in its paws, cracks the shell, and eats the nut meat.

Soon the squirrel finds another nut. This nut is starting to grow roots and would not be good to eat. The squirrel puts this nut back into the earth where it can keep growing. Someday the nut will be a fine tall tree.

Winter is coming soon. The gray squirrel will spend most of the winter in its nest high up in a tree. Every three or four days it will leave its warm nest to look for food. Down the tree the squirrel will go, looking for nuts stored in the ground.

During the summer, the gray squirrel had found many nuts and put them into the ground. It dug holes about three inches deep, one for each nut. It dropped each nut into a hole and then pushed the dirt back to cover it up. During the winter, the squirrel comes back to these holes for food.

How does the gray squirrel know where to find the nuts that were put into the ground earlier? The squirrel doesn't have to remember. Its nose does the work. Once the nut is found, the squirrel smells the nut to see if it is a good one. If the nut is good, the squirrel eats fast and hurries back home to its nest in the tree.

The gray squirrel is much safer in a tree than it is on the ground.

Ground Squirrel

The ground squirrel worries about winter. It also worries about summer. This squirrel can live almost anywhere, but it doesn't like very hot or very cold weather.

The ground squirrel lives beneath the ground. It digs a home so that it is safely hidden from other animals that might want to harm it. This squirrel also digs a storeroom for its food.

During the spring, the ground squirrel eats a lot of food and gets very fat. Because of all this fat, it can go for a long time without eating. When the very hot weather comes, the ground squirrel goes into its home beneath the ground and stays there. It waits for cooler weather.

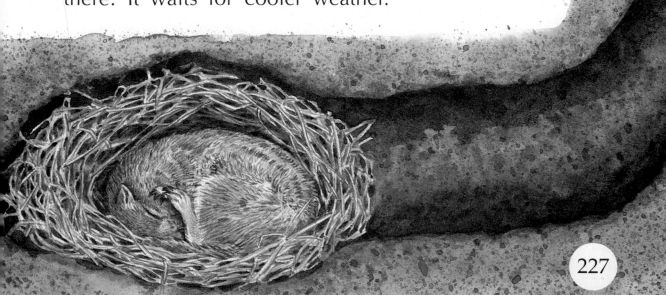

As soon as the weather gets cooler, the ground squirrel comes out from beneath the ground. Again it begins to gather food. This time the ground squirrel is getting ready for winter. The squirrel looks for nuts. It stuffs the nuts into a special pouch in its mouth and carries the nuts to its underground storeroom. It fills the storeroom with good food.

By the first snow of winter, the ground squirrel has grown very fat again. It hurries beneath the ground to its safe home. Then it curls up in a ball and goes to sleep. Sometimes it wakes up, but it doesn't need to go out for food. The food is right there in the storeroom. The ground squirrel doesn't even know about the wind and snow outside.

There are many other kinds of squirrels besides the gray squirrel and the ground squirrel. Even though the squirrels are different in some ways, they are all the same in two ways. All squirrels need safe places to live and food for the winter.

1. How are the two kinds of squirrels the same? How are they different?

2. Where do gray squirrels live? Where do ground squirrels live?

3. What do both kinds of squirrels do to get ready for winter?

4. Which kind of squirrel do you think is safer in winter?

5. What did you read that made you think that a gray squirrel has a good sense of smell?

Think and Write

Think about how people might get ready for a cold winter. Write a paragraph that tells three things people do to keep warm in winter.

Who is Betsy Ross? How did she use a needle to "fight for freedom"?

A Needle Fights for Freedom

by Esther MacLellan and Catherine V. Schroll

CHARACTERS

Peggy	**Mistress Betsy Ross**
Constance	**General Washington**
Elizabeth	**Robert Morris**
Anne	**Colonel Jones**
Prue	

Time: June 1776

Setting: Betsy Ross's home in Philadelphia. Girls are seated in a circle, sewing.

Peggy: *(jumping up)* In and out! In and out! Pushing a needle in and out! That's all you do when you're sewing.

Constance: My mother says every lady should be able to sew.

Elizabeth: So does mine.

Anne: There! I've stuck my finger again! Mean old needle!

Prue: My grandmother says we should be glad that Mistress Betsy Ross is teaching us to sew.

Peggy: Well, I'm not glad. I wish I were a boy. I'd join the army.

Prue: You're not big enough.

Peggy: I'm big enough to play a drum. *(pretends to beat a drum)* I'd be helping my country, too. How can you fight for freedom with a needle? *(Betsy Ross comes in.)*

Betsy Ross: Maybe you can't fight with a needle, Peggy, and maybe you can.

Peggy: Fight with a needle? How would a needle help our soldiers?

Betsy Ross: A needle makes warm clothes for the soldiers.

Peggy: I'm just sewing an old seam. I can't make clothes.

Betsy Ross: You never will be able to make clothes until you first learn on small things. Now show me your work. *(walks around the circle as she speaks)* Very nice, Prue. A little crooked, Anne. Peggy, your stitches are much too large.

Peggy: I wish they were even larger. Then I'd be finished.

Betsy Ross: Now you must rip out your seam and do it over.

Peggy: Again?

Betsy Ross: Again and again, until it's right. *(She leaves.)*

Constance: That's too bad, Peggy.

Peggy: *(sighing)* Well, I did hurry. If I were only helping in the fight for freedom, instead of just sewing! How I would love to do something for General Washington, something he really needed. *(sound of knocking is heard)*

Prue: Shall I answer the door?

Anne: Why not? Mistress Ross is busy in the kitchen. *(Prue goes to the door. General Washington, Robert Morris, and Colonel Jones come in.)*

Washington: Is this the home of Mistress Betsy Ross?

Prue: *(curtsying)* Yes, sir.

Peggy: *(rising)* Anne! Anne! That's General Washington!

Anne: You must be wrong, Peggy.

Peggy: Indeed I am not! *(to Washington)* Oh, sir, you *are* General Washington, aren't you?

Washington: *(bowing)* I am, indeed. *(Other men sit.)*

Peggy: But what are you doing *here,* sir? I thought you were busy.

Washington: *(smiling)* I *am* busy.

Peggy: I'm sorry, sir, I didn't mean you weren't. I meant busy in the army.

Washington: Not all the time, my dear.

Mr. Morris: Where is Mistress Ross?

Constance: I'll get her, sir. *(leaves)*

Mr. Morris: *(to Washington)* Are you sure that Mistress Ross will be able to do what we want?

Washington: I've heard that she is a fine needlewoman.

Elizabeth: Yes, sir, she is. Mistress Ross sews better than anyone else in Philadelphia.

Colonel Jones: Then she's the lady we want to meet. *(Betsy Ross comes in, followed by Constance.)*

Betsy Ross: *(curtsying)* General Washington! What a wonderful surprise, sir. What can I do for you?

Washington: Mistress Ross, this is Mr. Robert Morris and Colonel Jones.

Mr. Morris: *(bowing)* A pleasure, Mistress Ross.

Colonel Jones: *(bowing)* A pleasure.

Washington: We have come to ask you to do something important for your country.

235

Peggy: Is Mistress Ross to fight, sir?

Elizabeth: Peggy, do be quiet. General Washington will be angry.

Washington: Angry? Not I. There are other ways to help one's country. Mistress Ross can help us with her needle.

Colonel Jones: Mistress Ross, our country needs a flag.

Mr. Morris: Now that we are fighting England, we can no longer use the English flag that we once loved.

Colonel Jones: The colonies must have a flag of their own.

Washington: We need *one* flag for everybody. Then people will know that they are part of a new country.

Mr. Morris: They will know this is a free country, too, General Washington. All the colonies will be joined together under one great flag.

Betsy Ross: I shall do my best.

Washington: I am sure of it. These are our plans. *(takes paper from his pocket)* What do you think of this?

Betsy Ross: It's beautiful, General Washington. I like the thirteen stripes and thirteen stars.

Mr. Morris: Yes, a stripe and a star for each of the thirteen colonies.

Betsy Ross: *(pointing to plan)* This is the six-pointed star of the English flag. Let's have a new star for our new country. What do you say to a five-pointed star?

Washington: Would it be very hard to make?

Betsy Ross: Not at all, sir. Peggy, hand me your sewing, my child. *(pretends to cut and hold up a star)* How do you like the star, General Washington?

Washington: *(rising)* Very much. Mistress Ross, we will leave the plan with you.

Betsy Ross: I shall start at once.

Washington: Good!

Mr. Morris: Work fast, Mistress Ross. Our country needs its flag.

Washington: It does, indeed. Good-bye, Mistress Ross. *(to girls)* Good-bye, my dears. If you learn to sew as well as your good teacher, maybe one day your needles may help our country, too.

Betsy Ross: *(curtsying)* Good-bye, sir. *(The three men leave.)*

Peggy: To think my ugly old sewing would be the first star of our new flag!

Constance: *(waving her sewing)* I say that the needle that makes a flag is a needle that fights for freedom!

Peggy: *(slowly)* Well, I suppose you're right, Constance, though I still wish I could beat a drum. *(throws arms around Betsy Ross)* Even if I'm not very good at sewing, I'm very proud of my teacher.

Betsy Ross: Thank you, Peggy. Sewing class is over, girls. This very minute, I must start to make our first American flag!

Discuss the Selection

1. How did Betsy Ross use a needle to "fight for freedom"?

2. Why did General Washington ask Betsy Ross to make a new flag?

3. How did Peggy and Constance.feel about the making of a new flag? Why do you think they felt that way?

4. Find the words that tell how Peggy felt about the fight for freedom.

Think and Write

The girls had to learn to sew seams before they could make clothes. What things would you have to learn to do before you would be able to make a meal? Make a list of those things.

Follow Directions
Make a Star Mobile

In "A Needle Fights for Freedom," Betsy Ross was asked to use a plan to make a new flag for America. Sometimes you may make something from a plan, too. Often there are written directions to follow. These directions may have two or more steps.

When you are going to follow written directions, here are some things you should do.

1. Gather everything you need.
2. Read through all the steps.
   Then read them again.
3. Be sure you understand each step.
4. Follow each step in order.

Listed below are directions for making a star mobile. The first set of directions tells how to make the stars. The second set of directions tells how to put the stars together to make a mobile.

To Make the Stars

Things you will need: paper, pencil, scissors

1. On a piece of paper, draw a star to use as a pattern.

2. Cut out the pattern.

3. On another piece of paper, trace the pattern eight times.

4. Cut out the eight stars. This will give you four pairs of stars.

To Make the Mobile

Things you will need: stars, scissors, enough yarn for four ten-inch pieces, glue, coat hanger

1. Cut four pieces of yarn, one piece for each pair of stars. Each piece of yarn should be ten inches long.

2. Lay one star from each pair on the table.

3. Glue a piece of yarn to each star on the table.

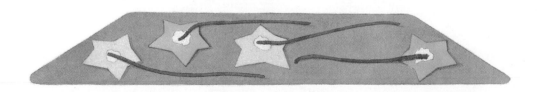

4. Take the second star of each pair and put it on top of the first star, yarn, and glue. You have glued the two stars together. Do this for each star pair. When you have finished, you will have four star pairs.

5. Tie the other end of each piece of yarn to the coat hanger. You may wish to tie the yarn so that some pieces are shorter than others.

You have made a star mobile!

Like Betsy Ross, Mary McDonald helped her country in a very special way during the Revolutionary War. What does Mary do?

Thanks to Mary

by Ann Bixby Herold

Mary McDonald was a young girl during the Revolutionary War. She worried about the hungry soldiers with General Washington at Valley Forge. Mary worked in a big house where there was lots of food. She began to think of what she could do to help the soldiers.

Every time Mary sat down to eat, she
thought about the soldiers. She had
plenty to eat, and they were hungry.
She had warm clothes to wear, and
they were cold. It worried her more
and more.

She started to save some of her food—
some nuts here, an apple there. Then
she took the food she had saved to
General Washington's tent. "I'm Mary
McDonald. I've come to join the army,"
she told the soldier standing there.

"You? Girls can't join the army."

"I've brought some food," said Mary, as she handed him an apple.

The soldier smiled down at her. "Follow me, miss," he said. He took her to Mrs. Washington. "Mary McDonald is here to join the army, ma'am," he said.

Mrs. Washington smiled at Mary. "We have need of busy hands," she said.

There was plenty of work for Mary to do. She sewed. She knitted. She carried baskets of food to the sick soldiers.

Mary also ran messages. No one ever stopped or questioned her. She could carry messages to places a grown-up could not go.

Hurrying along an icy path early one morning, Mary's sharp eyes noticed something high in a tree. It was a man dressed all in brown. He was staring out over the camp.

He hadn't seen Mary, so she went for a closer look. She moved up the hill from tree to tree. She was careful to walk only on the bare patches that matched her brown cloak.

The man had a telescope. He was staring through the telescope and writing things down. He looked well fed and warmly dressed. Mary was sure he didn't come from Valley Forge. "A British spy!" she thought.

Quietly Mary slipped away. When she reached the icy path again, she slipped and fell. The man heard her. He looked down the hill. Then he turned away. Why should he worry about a little girl?

Mary hurried back to camp. She told an officer that she had seen a British spy. The officer at Valley Forge sent four soldiers back with Mary. The man was too busy spying on the camp to see them making their way up the hill. The soldiers made Mary hide behind a rock while they went to catch the spy.

Mary became a hero. The officers in camp all raised their hats when Mary walked by. The soldiers saluted her. Someone even heard General Washington say, "If I had more soldiers like Mary McDonald, this war would be over."

This made-up story is based on fact. General Washington's army did camp at Valley Forge in the winter of 1777–1778. The army was short of food and clothes. Martha Washington spent much of the winter at the camp. She and the other women took food to the soldiers. They fixed clothes. They took care of the sick. The women at the camp tried to help the soldiers as much as they could.

1. Name three things that Mary did to help her country.
2. Why could Mary come and go with messages?
3. Why did the soldiers salute Mary when she walked by?
4. How did you feel when Mary slipped and fell?
5. Where in the story did you know how the soldiers felt about Mary after she had helped to catch the spy?

Think about how Mary helped the soldiers long ago. Write a paragraph that tells what you could do to help grown-ups today.

This story is from the book The Wonderful Wizard of Oz. *Read to find out about some of the characters Dorothy meets as she tries to find the Wizard.*

from The Wonderful Wizard of Oz

by L. Frank Baum

Dorothy and her dog, Toto, are in the Land of Oz. Dorothy wants very much to get back home to Kansas. She and Toto are looking for the Wonderful Wizard of Oz. She thinks he will help them.

Dorothy knows that the Wizard of Oz lives in the Emerald City. She is on her way there when she meets the Scarecrow.

Dorothy was surprised to see one of the Scarecrow's eyes slowly wink at her.

"Good day," said the Scarecrow, in a low voice.

"Did you speak?" asked the girl.

"Certainly," replied the Scarecrow. "How do you do?"

"I'm pretty well, thank you," said Dorothy, politely. "How do you do?"

"I'm not feeling well," said the Scarecrow, with a smile. "It is very tiring being perched up here night and day to scare away crows."

"Can't you get down?" asked Dorothy.

"No. I am stuck on this pole. If you will please take me off the pole, I shall be thankful."

Dorothy reached up both arms and lifted the Scarecrow off the pole. Because he was stuffed with straw, the Scarecrow was quite light.

"Thank you very much," said the Scarecrow, when he had been set down on the ground. "I feel like a new man."

Dorothy was puzzled at this. It was strange to hear a stuffed man speak, and to see him try to stand straight.

"Who are you?" asked the Scarecrow, when he had stretched himself. "Where are you going?"

"My name is Dorothy," said the girl. "I am going to the Emerald City, to ask the great Oz to send me back to Kansas."

"Where is the Emerald City?" he asked. "Who is Oz?"

"Why, don't you know?" she replied in surprise.

"No, indeed. I don't know anything. You see, I am stuffed. I have no brains at all," he replied sadly.

"Oh," said Dorothy. "I'm so very sorry for you."

"Do you think," he asked, "that if I go to the Emerald City with you, the great Oz would give me some brains?"

"I cannot tell," she said, "but you may come with me, if you like. If Oz will not give you any brains, you will be no worse off than you are now."

"No worse, that is true," said the Scarecrow. "You see," he continued, "I don't mind my legs and arms and body being stuffed, because I can't get hurt. If anyone walks on my toes or sticks a pin into me, it doesn't matter. I can't feel it. I do not want people to call me a fool, though. If my head stays stuffed with straw, instead of with brains as yours is, how am I ever to know anything?"

"I understand how you feel," said
Dorothy, who was really sorry for him.
"If you will come with me, I'll ask Oz to
do all he can for you."

"Thank you," said the Scarecrow.

They walked back to the road. Dorothy
helped him over the fence. They started
along the yellow brick road to the
Emerald City.

Toto, Dorothy's little dog, did not like
the Scarecrow at first. He smelled around
the stuffed Scarecrow and growled at him.

259

"Don't mind Toto," said Dorothy to her new friend. "He never bites."

"Oh, I'm not afraid," replied the Scarecrow. "He can't hurt the straw. Do let me carry that basket for you. I shall not mind it, for I can't get tired. I'll tell you a secret," he continued, as they walked along. "There is only one thing in the world I am afraid of."

"What is that?" asked Dorothy. "Is it the farmer who made you?"

"No," answered the Scarecrow. "It's a lighted match."

Dorothy and the Scarecrow continued on their journey to the Emerald City and the Wizard of Oz. On the way they met the Tin Woodman and the Cowardly Lion.

The Tin Woodman and the Cowardly Lion wanted to see the Wonderful Wizard of Oz, too. The Tin Woodman wanted Oz to give him a heart. The Cowardly Lion wanted Oz to give him courage.

They had many adventures on the way to the Emerald City. Now they are close to it. All they must do is find the yellow brick road in the Land of Oz again. It will take them to the Emerald City, where the great Oz lives.

It was not long before Dorothy and
her friends came to the yellow brick
road. Soon they began to see fences and
houses. They were all painted green. All
the people were dressed in green clothes.
No one came near them because everyone
was afraid of the Cowardly Lion.

"This must be the Land of Oz," said
Dorothy. "We must be getting near the
Emerald City."

"Yes," said the Scarecrow. "The people
do not seem very friendly, though. I am
afraid we will not find a place to stay
for the night."

"I should like something to eat," said Dorothy. "I'm sure Toto is hungry, too. Let's stop at the next house and talk to the people."

When they came to a farm house, Dorothy walked right up to the door and knocked. A woman opened the door just far enough to look out and said, "What do you want, child? Why is that lion with you?"

"We wish to spend the night with you, if we may," said Dorothy. "The lion is my friend. He would not hurt you for the world."

"Is he tame?" asked the woman, opening the door a little wider.

"Oh, yes," said the girl. "He is a great coward, too. He will be more afraid of you than you are of him."

263

"Well," said the woman, after thinking it over and taking another look at the Cowardly Lion. "If that is so, you may come in, and I will give you something to eat and a place to sleep."

They all went into the house. Inside there were two children and a man. The man asked, "Where are you all going?"

"We are going to the Emerald City," said Dorothy. "We are going to see the Great Oz."

"Oh!" said the man. "Are you sure that Oz will see you?"

"Why not?" asked Dorothy.

"It is said that he never lets anyone near. I have been to the Emerald City many times. It is a beautiful and wonderful place, but I've never seen the Great Oz. I don't know anyone who has."

"Does he never go out?" asked the Scarecrow.

"That is hard to tell," said the man. "You see, Oz is a great Wizard. He can take any shape he wants. Some say he looks like a bird. Some say he looks like an elephant. Some say he looks like a cat. Who the real Oz is, when he is in his own shape, no one can tell."

"That is very strange," said Dorothy. "We must try, in some way, to see him, or we shall have made our journey for nothing."

"Why do you wish to see Oz?" asked the man.

"I want him to give me some brains," said the Scarecrow.

"Oh, Oz could do that," said the man. "He has more brains than he needs."

"I want him to give me a heart," said the Tin Woodman.

"That will not trouble him," said the man. "Oz has a large number of hearts, of all sizes and shapes."

"I want him to give me courage," said the Cowardly Lion.

"Oz keeps a great pot of courage in his room," said the man. "He will be glad to give you some."

"I want him to send me back to Kansas," said Dorothy.

"Where is Kansas?" asked the man.

"I don't know," said Dorothy, sadly. "It is my home, though. I'm sure it's somewhere."

"Well, Oz can do anything. I suppose he will find Kansas for you. First, however, you must get to see him."

The next morning, as soon as the sun was up, they started out. Soon they saw a beautiful green light in the sky just before them. "That must be the Emerald City," said Dorothy.

At the gate to the city, a man gave them special glasses because the green of the Emerald City might hurt their eyes. Then he took a big gold key and opened another gate. They all followed him through the gate into the Emerald City.

1. What characters did Dorothy meet? Why did each one want to see Oz?

2. Why did Dorothy want to see the Wizard of Oz?

3. Why do you think the Scarecrow is afraid of a lighted match?

4. Why doesn't anyone know what the Great Oz looks like?

5. How did you feel when Dorothy and her friends went through the gates to the city? Why?

6. When in the story did you think that the people at the farm were afraid of Dorothy and her friends?

Thinking About "Patterns"

Everything you have read in this unit had something to do with a pattern. A pattern, you remember, is something that is repeated over and over again.

You read fables, which have been told for years and years. You read made-up stories set in real times from the past. You read about the two grandfathers and the two squirrels who lived their lives by a pattern.

As you read other stories, think about whether or not the characters fit into a pattern. Then think about whether the stories might fit into a unit called "Patterns."

1. How are the stories "City Mouse and Country Mouse" and "City Grandfather, Country Grandfather" the same? How are they different?

2. Is the ant or the grasshopper more like the squirrel at work? Why?

3. Think of a character from this unit who might have wanted to see the Wizard of Oz. What would that character have asked for? Why?

4. Which character's life had the most interesting pattern? Why do you think so?

Read on Your Own

Animals in Winter by Henrietta Bancroft and Richard G. Van Gelder. Harper. This book tells how animals get ready for and live through the winter months.

The Wizard of Oz by L. Frank Baum. Holt. This book tells the whole story of Dorothy and her friends in the Land of Oz.

How to Have Fun Making Mobiles. Childrens Press. Learn how to make hanging mobiles and mobiles on stands. The mobiles can be made with paper, sticks, wood, or clay.

Town and Country by Alice and Martin Provensen. Crown. This book shows what life is like in a big city and on a country farm. There are many beautiful pictures.

The Tortoise and the Hare by Janet Stevens. Holiday. This is an old story retold. This tortoise wears sneakers. The hare wears running shorts.

Alexander Who Used to Be Rich Last Sunday by Judith Viorst. Atheneum. Alexander can't understand how his money gets used up so quickly.

If I Were in Charge of the World and Other Worries by Judith Viorst. Atheneum. This book has poems about things such as wishes, worries, words, and nights.

Baby Bear and the Long Sleep by Andrew Ward. Little, Brown. Baby Bear has trouble settling down for the long winter sleep.

Squirrels by Brian Wildsmith. Watts. This book tells what squirrels are like, what they do, and where they live.

Glossary

The glossary is a special dictionary for this book. To find a word, use alphabetical, or ABC, order. For example, to find the word *swing* in the glossary, first look for the part of the glossary that has words beginning with the letter *s.* Then find the entry word, *swing.* The glossary gives the meaning of the word as it is used in the book. Then the word is used in a sentence.

Sometimes different forms of the word follow the sentence. If a different form of the word, such as *swung,* is used in the book, then that word is used in the sentence.

A small blue box ■ at the end of the entry means that there is a picture to go with that word.

A

above over: She could not reach the basketball net high *above* her.

B

backyard a yard behind a house: A good place to play is in the *backyard*. ■

bare without covering: In the winter the trees were *bare*.

bend to turn or move in a different direction: To get through the door, the tall man must *bend* down.
bending, bent

beneath under: The banging came from the room *beneath* us.

bleed to lose blood: The cut on his arm is *bleeding*.
bleeding, bled

blink to open and close the eyes quickly: She *blinked* when she took off on her first flight.
blinked, blinking

block the land with streets on four sides: My house is the last one on the *block*.

booth a small space with three walls: The children made a *booth* in which to sell old toys. ■

boss a person that people take orders from: He wanted to be *boss* of the program.

brain place in the head where thoughts take place: People have bigger *brains* than animals. **brains**

breath air that goes in and out of the body: She took a deep *breath* before she jumped in the water.

brick pieces of baked clay: Most of the buildings in town are made of *brick.*

bunch a group of the same things that belong together: Mother will pick a *bunch* of grapes for us to eat.

businessman a man who works at a business: The *businessman* sold many tractors to farmers to use on the land.

C

---

cake a baked food: She made a large *cake* for a birthday surprise.

camp a group of tents: The soldiers were in a *camp* by the river. ■

chair a place to sit: She sat on a *chair* in the very first row. There were eight rows of *chairs* in the small room. **chairs**

chop to cut with a tool: He will *chop* the meat. They are *chopping* the carrots. **chopping, chopped**

clank to make the sound of metal hitting: The door will *clank* when it opens. The gate *clanked* as it hit the pole. **clanked**

classmate someone in the same class: He went to the museum with his *classmates*. **classmates**

cling to hold tightly: The caterpillar will *cling* to the stick. **clung, clinging**

cloak a long cape: The girl pulled the long *cloak* tightly around her to keep warm. ■

cool not warm: There was a *cool* wind out at sea.

crooked not straight: The line he drew was too *crooked* to use as a frame for the picture.

crow a black bird: The *crow* flew down to pick up the seeds from the garden.

curl to bend into a round shape: The snake *curls* around the tree. **curls, curled** ■

D

deed a thing that is done: The boy's brave *deeds* saved the town. **deeds**

die to stop living: Her pet frog *died* before she moved out of town. **died, dies**

dining room a place to eat meals: The people took their food to the *dining room*.

dirt loose earth: We drive to the farm on a *dirt* road.

downtown in the middle of town: Most of the people work in the buildings *downtown*.

drawing artwork done by using lines: The artist showed his *drawings* at an art show. **drawings**

drum an instrument that is hit to make music: She played the *drum* in the band. ▪

dull having no excitement: She went to sleep during the *dull* show.

dumb not smart: It is *dumb* to play in the street.

dust fine dirt: The chairs had a covering of *dust*.

E
---

earlier coming before: He walked quickly and was at school *earlier* than his friends.

F
---

fade to become less bright: The color *faded* when the dress was washed. **faded**

fair being the same for all: It is not *fair* when one person is first all the time.

flat in a smooth, even way: He fell *flat* on his back.

flight a trip made by flying: The plane made a *flight* from one country to another country far away.

flop to jump down in a heavy way: The boys *flopped* on the bed. **flopped, flopping**

fog   a cloud near the ground: They did not see the people jogging in the *fog*. ■

fool   a silly person: He acted like a *fool*.

forget   to not remember: The sailor must have *forgotten* where he put the boat. **forgot, forgotten**

G
---

gold   a yellow metal used as money: She put all of her *gold* in the bank.

grab   to catch something and hold on hard: He *grabbed* the rope so they could pull him from the water. **grabbed, grabbing**

grade   a step in order: He is in the *grade* above me.

grape   a kind of fruit: The *grapes* grew in the backyard. **grapes** ■

gray   a color made by mixing black and white: The girl's new dress was *gray*.

grin   a big smile: They *grinned* when the clowns got out of the van. **grinned, grinning**

growl   to make an angry sound: The dog *growled* when the man came over the fence. **growled, growling**

279

H

hardworking doing a job that is hard: The *hardworking* detective went after the robber.

harm to hurt: The fire did not *harm* the barn.

hay dry grass: They took the *hay* into the barn to feed the animals.

headline words with heavy letters at the top of a newspaper story: The *headlines* were about the basketball game. **headlines**

heel the back part of the foot: It is hard to walk on your *heels*. **heels** ■

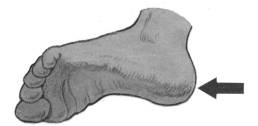

hut a small house: The woman lived in a *hut* in the forest.

J

jar a bottle with a wide top: He put his brush in the paint *jar*. ■

jog to run slowly: The boys went *jogging* every day after school. **jogging, jogged**

K

known to have learned about: She said she had *known* the poem for a long time.

L

lady a woman: The *lady* had gray curls all over her head.

leg a part of the body that people and animals use to stand: He put one *leg* over the fence. ■

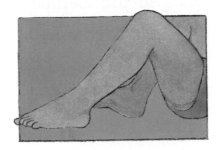

lick to pass the tongue over: At first the dog would only *lick* the bone.

lift to raise up: The wind *lifted* the kite over the trees. **lifted**

lip the edge of the mouth: The snow made his *lips* cold. **lips** ■

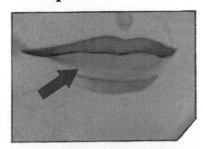

lock to join: We will *lock* hands before we climb the hill.

match **1.** to be like: The girls in the class had *matching* hats. **2.** to find things that look the same: She wanted to *match* the red in the picture. **matching**

meal food to eat at a certain time of day: Our friends often eat a *meal* with us.

neck the part of the body that holds up the head: I put a rope around the horse's *neck*. ■

nest a home made by an animal: Small birds may live in a *nest* until they fly.

O
---

oil to put oil on: She *oiled* the parts of the machine before she used it. **oiled**

P
---

pant to take fast breaths: After chasing the cat, the dog lay down and *panted*. **panted, panting**

patch a small piece of cloth used to cover a hole: She used parts of old dresses as *patches*. **patches** ■

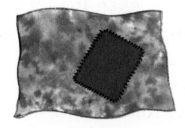

peanut seed from a certain plant which is eaten: At the circus, people feed *peanuts* to the elephants. **peanuts**

peek to take a fast look at: She opened the door a little bit to *peek* outside. **peeked**

perch to sit: The owl *perched* in the tree all night. **perched**

pip a dot on a domino: She looked for a domino with two *pips*. **pips**

plate a flat dish: He must eat all the food on his *plate*. ■

popcorn corn that is popped open by heat: We buy *popcorn* at the carnival.

pouch a little bag: The man put his gold in a *pouch*. ■

prize a reward for something: Her pictures won two *prizes* at the art show. **prizes**

proud feeling good about something: I am *proud* to be on the team.

punch a fruit drink: She filled the glasses with *punch* for her party.

Q

quietly with little sound: You may play the music if you play it *quietly*, so that it doesn't bother anyone.

R

reach to stretch to get something: He had to jump up to *reach* the ball that went over his head.

rich having a lot of money: Sometimes *rich* people live in castles.

rule a way something must be done: My mother's *rule* is that everyone must help.

S

scold to talk sharply to someone: He was *scolding* her for making a hole in his kite. **scolding**

seam a line where pieces of cloth are put together: He cut open the *seam* to make the costume bigger.

seat a place to sit: The woman was glad to find a *seat* on the bus.

serve to bring something to someone: I will *serve* you a sandwich for lunch.

shelf a flat piece of wood on a wall: All the books were put on a *shelf* over the desk. ■

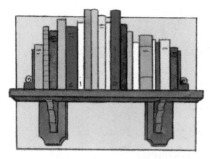

shell a hard covering: The turtle has a *shell* on its back.

shoot to throw: At the game, everyone wanted to *shoot* the ball into the basket. **shot, shooting**

shy easy to frighten: She was too *shy* to sing for all the people.

sidewalk a path at the side of a street: The van was on the road near the *sidewalk*.

sight how far away a person can see: She watched until the bird was no longer in *sight*.

skateboard a piece of wood on small wheels: He rolled down the hill on his *skateboard*. ■

smooth to make even: She *smoothed* the bed after the dog flopped on it. **smoothed**

sniff to take short breaths through the nose: They *sniffed* the air when they came near the flowers. **sniffed**

snug safe and warm: The robins were *snug* in their winter home.

284

soak to make very wet: He *soaks* the grass with a hose. **soaks**

sob to cry hard: The little boy *sobbed* when the barber began to cut his hair. **sobbed**

soil ground where plants grow: The farmer puts seeds in the *soil* every spring.

spacecraft something in which people travel away from Earth: The *spacecraft* will carry the people far away from our planet. ■

speak to talk: She shows excitement when she *speaks* about her new school. **speaks**

spend to use or use up: They will *spend* some time at the zoo.

spoon something often used to eat soft foods: He ate the hot cereal with one of the small *spoons*. **spoons** ■

spread to put out over a large space: They *spread* out the newspapers to keep the paint off the floor. **spreading**

spy 1. a person who finds out secrets: The man hiding under the bridge is a *spy*. 2. to find out the secrets of others: The new woman at the store is *spying* on the owner. **spying**

285

stack   **1.** to pile up: The man began to *stack* the boxes in the truck. **2.** a pile: Soon the boxes made a large *stack.* ■

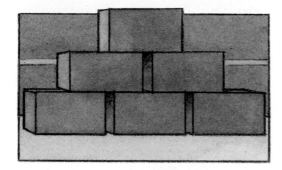

steep   going up suddenly: It was hard for the people to climb the *steep* hill.

stick   **1.** a long thin piece of wood: He used a *stick* as a cane. 2. to put in: He *stuck* his hand in the hole to get the cat. **stuck, sticking**

stitch   spot where thread and cloth are joined together: He used large *stitches* to sew up his jeans. **stitches**

storeroom   a room where many things are kept: The people put all their food in the *storeroom.*

stream   a small river: Everyone wanted to catch fish in the *stream.* ■

streetlight   a light on a tall pole that shines light over the street: It was not dark in the city, because there were many *streetlights.*

stretch   to reach far: He began each day by *stretching* to help him wake up. **stretching, stretched**

stripe   a line of a different color: She painted a blue *stripe* on the boat.

summertime   the days that follow spring: Everyone likes to go for a swim in the *summertime.*

sweep   to clean away with a broom: She *swept* the leaves that fell from the tree into the street.
swept, sweeping

T

---

tame   used to living with people: The horse in the barn is so *tame* that you will be able to walk right up and pat its head.

tent   a covering on poles, used for shelter: On the trip everyone wanted to sleep in the *tent.* ■

thankful   happy about something good: They were *thankful* when the truck came to a stop before it hit the house.

tomorrow   the day after today: Everyone will come *tomorrow.*

tonight   this night: The celebration will start *tonight.*

trunk   an elephant's nose: At the circus we saw an elephant pick up a man with its *trunk.* ■

twin   one of two children born at the same time to the same mother: The boy and his *twin* looked alike.

287

two-wheeler a bike with two wheels: She rode to school on her shiny new *two-wheeler*. ■

wag to swish from side to side: The dog *wagged* its tail when the children came. **wagged, wagging** ■

U

underground in the earth: The dog hid his bone *underground*.

V

vote to choose as a group: The children *voted* to make the dog their class pet. **voted, voting**

wear to have on the body: She *wore* a clown costume at the party. **wore, wearing**

wheel to move on wheels: She will *wheel* her bike to the back of the house.

wipe to rub: She used her hand as she *wiped* the rain from her face. **wiped, wiping**

worse less good: The rain was *worse* than the snow.

Word List

The following words are introduced in this book. Each is listed beside the number of the page on which it first appears.

Illustrators

Lynn Uhde-Adams: 242–245; Mike Adams: 114–115, 224–228; Bill/Judie Anderson: 50–56, 106–107; Ray App: 64–72, 130–138; Ellen Appleby: 30–31, 42–43, 140; Allen Atkinson: 194–202; Alex Bloch: 22–28; Susan Brooks: 254–268; Eulala Conner: 12–13; Dee Deloy: 104–105; Don Dyen: 173; Larry Frederick: 246–252; Bob Jackson: 210–211; Gary Lippencott: 204–208; Ken Longtemps: 92–102; Larry Mikec: 4–10; Bill Ogden: 156–157; Bev Pardee: 160–170, 212–213; Jerry Pinkney: 142–148, 172; Tom Powers: 109, 112; Don Siculan: 230–240; Blanche Sims: 76–84, 214; John Slobodnick: 158–159; Jozef Sumichrast: 216–222.

HBJ maps and charts: pp. 20, 74.

8
9
E 0
F 1
G 2
H 3
I 4
J 5